Y0-CMO-577

Publications on Asia of the
Institute for Comparative and Foreign Area Studies
Number 23

This book is sponsored by the South Asian Program of the Institute for Comparative and Foreign Area Studies (formerly Far Eastern and Russian Institute).

श्रीः

Studies in the Language and Culture of South Asia

EDITED BY EDWIN GEROW AND MARGERY D. LANG

UNIVERSITY OF WASHINGTON PRESS

Seattle and London

DISCARDED
WIDENER UNIVERSITY
WIDENER COLLEGE
WOLFGRAM LIBRARY
CHESTER, PA.
150007

Copyright © 1973 by the University of Washington Press
Printed in the United States of America

All rights reserved. No part of this publication may be reproduced or transmitted in any form or by any means, electronic or mechanical, including photocopy, recording, or any information storage or retrieval system, without permission in writing from the publisher.

Library of Congress Cataloging in Publication Data
Main entry under title:
Studies in the language and culture of South Asia.
(Publications on Asia of the Institute for Comparative and Foreign Area Studies, no. 23)
Papers presented at a summer seminar held at the University of Washington in 1969.
Includes bibliographical references.
1. India—Civilization—Congresses. 2. Indic philology—Congresses. I. Gerow, Edwin, ed. II. Lang, Margery D., ed. III. Series: Washington (State). University. Institute for Comparative and Foreign Area Studies. Publications on Asia, no. 23.
DS423.S85 1974 915.4'03 73-18028
ISBN 0-295-95316-0

Publications on Asia of the Institute for Comparative and Foreign Area Studies is a continuation of the series formerly entitled Far Eastern and Russian Institute Publications on Asia.

Foreword

It is a special pleasure to introduce the first publication sponsored by the South Asian Program of the Institute for Comparative and Foreign Area Studies of the University of Washington. The appearance of this publication marks an important stage in the development of the program, which has grown rapidly in recent years to become one of the major area studies programs of the Institute. The Institute has sponsored the publication of twenty-five volumes in its two series, one on Asia and one on Russia and Eastern Europe. With this volume, the Asian series is enlarging to include South Asia, reflecting the size and vigor of the South Asian Program.

Herbert J. Ellison
Director
Institute for Comparative and Foreign Area Studies
University of Washington

Contents

Introduction		ix
Two Indian Novels of Partition: *Mano Majra* and *Jhutha Sach*	*Usha Nilsson*	3
Vaikom Muhammad Basheer	*Ronald E. Asher*	19
Alienation in the Modern Hindi Short Story	*Gordon C. Roadarmel*	48
Faith and Love in Bengali Poetry	*Edward Dimock*	63
Devi Shrines and Folk Hinduism in Medieval Tamilnad	*Burton Stein*	75
Prolegomenon to a Cultural History of the Gangetic Civilization	*Barrie M. Morrison*	91
Some Thoughts on Indian Government Policy as It Affects Sanskrit Education	*Edwin Gerow*	111
Language, Linguistics, and Politics in Tamilnad	*Harold Schiffman*	125
Caste Ranking: Sacred-Secular, Tails, and Dogs	*Martin Orans*	135
The Multileveled Ontology of Advaita Vedānta	*Eliot Deutsch*	151

Introduction

The present volume of essays is noteworthy on three counts. For the University of Washington, it represents the first publication on South Asia to receive the imprimatur of the Institute for Comparative and Foreign Area Studies, recognizing the wider area focus of this long-established and prestigious body.

For the federally supported programs of summer language study, the volume represents the productive utility of bringing together a distinguished faculty able not only to teach, but themselves to profit from what became a three-month intensive seminar on problems of language and culture in South Asia. Seven of these papers stem from the faculty itself; three are those of guests invited for the purpose.

For the papers that resulted, a coherently high quality distinguishes the volume, and again reflects favorably on the utility of the format that brought the writers together for a sustained exchange of views.

These papers are not simply the collected lectures of gentlemen brought at random to a campus; they emerged from a single program and reflect the intensity and focus of that program. In bringing out this set of essays, it is my purpose not so much to praise the quality of the individual contributions, which is self-evident, but to call attention to the program that provoked them and made them possible.

The National Defense Education Act-supported summer language-training programs were, from 1963 until 1971, a regular feature of foreign area studies programs. In recent years they have been increasingly administered through cooperative consortia of interested universities; cooperation has not only augmented the quality of the summer programs but eliminated duplication and waste of dispersed resources. A truly national consensus was emerging in the late sixties that presumed and encouraged comprehensive planning of resource allocation on a national basis for the first time. The summer programs were in this sense a testing ground of possibilities that should have had major impact on the full-year programs of the participating universities.

In South Asian studies, three national consortia had emerged, the newest grouping several western and far-western schools, including Texas, Berkeley, Washington, and Hawaii. The latter group also tried to include for the first time a Canadian school, the University of British Columbia, but federal laws made this otherwise desirable international association most difficult to work out in administrative detail.

The intensive summer language-training program was conceived in 1963 as supplement to the regular academic year offerings of the constituent area studies programs, mostly funded by NDEA Title VI, and reflected the view that such intensive training, especially on the elementary level, could, if offered consistently during the summers, both augment the language training of regularly enrolled students in area centers and make such training more widely available to students in universities where no area or language work was available during the academic year.

These purposes continued to be served throughout the history of the summer sessions, but were associated with other goals, originally ancillary or accidental, which more and more assumed the role of central justifications of the whole summer-session program. It is this new orientation that is presented in this volume of studies; one that I think should be emphasized in the current debate over the future of summer language programs.

Without in any way compromising the integrity of the language teaching component, successful summer programs have more and more emphasized area studies, and—most interestingly—not on the elementary level, but on the advanced and graduate levels, through a faculty of real distinction brought together for that purpose. The extended program thus served two related and inimitable functions: intensive graduate training with specialists not normally available to the student, augmented and structured contacts of expert faculty associating in pursuit of related interests. A kind of hothouse effect was palpable, and for those participating, became a measure of the benefit derived.

This volume is composed of papers presented at one such summer program seminar, held at the University of Washington in 1969. The 1969 program in fact inaugurated the Western States Consortium in South Asian studies; this volume was originally conceived as evidence for the promotion and encouragement of similar programs to be sponsored by other participating universities. With the drastic curtailment in NDEA funding in 1971, and the consequent withdrawal of all support for such summer programs in the United States, a very different perspective has emerged, in which—obviously—the basic questions of utility and survival of summer programs themselves are posed. In a way, the present volume is a more eloquent argument to the latter issue than to the former, for the contributors have established here not only the quality and uniqueness of the program they staffed, but have shown, by their counterexample, how much is lost when the possibility of such efforts ceases. It is especially important that the question be faced in these terms, not according to the parochial and outdated rationales of the early sixties.

The focus of this seminar was on Indian language and culture. Though the terms of reference were necessarily vague, so as to encourage the most thoughtful and personal contributions of each participant, each essay reflects a position within that limited set of parameters, and together, they help to define the interrelations and limits of the broader issue itself.

The arrangement of the essays reflects a logic of literary development through the specifics of history to the universals of culture. In turn, the many integral facets of the cultural problem demonstrate the need of many critical stances in adapting the intransigent facts of behavior to the luminous word of understanding. Our logic perhaps compels us to begin with poetry, as that form of language most directly imbued with the experience of man; still we do not, but are content to call attention to the poetic spirit that illuminates the scholarly method of many of these essays.

Usha Nilsson (University of Wisconsin), a novelist and critic, treats of a climactic historic event—partition—as measure and test of two novels that bear firsthand witness to its horror.

Ronald E. Asher (University of Edinburgh) concentrates on the life work of one Malayali writer—Basheer—a Muslim, and attempts to define there a very un-Indian kind of contemporary realism: unabashed autobiography.

Gordon Roadarmel (late of the University of California, Berkeley) probes the anti-historicism of much of modern Hindi literature to assess the psychic reality behind the stereotypes of the collapsing *dharmic* ideal. His writers explore the homelessness of the modern "individual" who seeks outwardly to establish himself as valid in confrontation *with* the "meaningless" past, but inwardly often fails for want of resources that are supplied only by that past.

Edward Dimock (University of Chicago) writes of themes of faith and love in Bengali poetry, and explores the incestuous relationship of poetry and religion: poetry achieves its finest tones in the service of devotion; devotion itself becomes the poetic act par excellence. In isolation, however, poetry is insipid bawdy and religion is increasingly unrefined ritual. And these ideal moments seem to characterize the evolution of Bengali Vaiṣṇava poetry before the coming of the British.

Like the *bhaktas* of Bengal, who realize in ever-present song the presence of Rādhā and her lover Kṛṣṇa, *Burton Stein* (University of Hawaii) demonstrates the *avatāra* of the *dēvī* among the *bhaktas* of medieval South India. With Stein's paper, the focus of the essays shifts slightly to the cultural context conditioning the origin and development of literate traditions.

Barrie M. Morrison (University of British Columbia) zeroes in on communication itself—transmission of culture through time—as a node of cultural organization with its own structure and conventions. His essay helps to understand and clarify the implications of the specific study that follows—that of

Edwin Gerow (University of Washington), who appraises the increasing social and political obstacles to the transmission of the historically most central literate tradition of India, that of the orthodox Sanskritist.

Harold Schiffman (University of Washington) examines the inverse of the same question, documenting the modalities of imposing on a growing modern language political myths that purport to validate an imaginary past.

Martin Orans (University of California, Riverside) broadens the discussion from method of culture to theory of culture, seeking to clarify the current discussion of caste and hierarchy, notions that define the essential character of Indian society as a specific world culture. And really not too far from Orans in point of view is

Eliot Deutsch (University of Hawaii) who, like the Vedāntin, leaps beyond society to a theory of hierarchy itself, a hierarchy of being whose metaphysical implications for the Indian social order were as apparent to Śaṁkara as they are to us today. At this most general level we have seemingly lost sight of the traumas that began this volume: "partition" as defined by particular historical novels. For those who still dispute the central coherence of these essays in their topical variety, I recommend consideration of the final sentences of Eliot Deutsch's paper, which also end this book. His observation applies to the collection itself.

It is unfortunate that the discussions these papers provoked could not also be set forth here; they were an integral and increasingly useful part of the seminar—particularly for the participating faculty, who had to adjust to a perspective different from that of their home institutions.

The range is great, but in each effort, the tension between expression—be it literary, philosophical, or scientific—and its volatile cultural reference, is clear. Perhaps we have in microcosm captured the most important thing that can be said about Indian society, that it is a persistent culture, has been the world's most consistent civilizing force, and is thus a precondition and a stimulus to a major part of man's literary expression.

In editing these essays, I have not tried to impose on them an artificial uniformity of punctuation or style. Indian terms are rendered according to a common diacritical system applying to that language, except when the author clearly chooses to use them as English words (as often, "Cochin," not "Koẓikoḍe"). Dr. Asher's Anglicisms have not been excised in deference to our common mother, *Āṅglabhāṣā*.

Postscript. Gordon Roadarmel's study here published is one of the last, and best, pieces in his literary bequest. I have had to assume responsibility for its final form. In this sensitive and disturbing essay, it often seemed to me that Gordon spoke much of himself—much more perhaps than those of us who heard it knew. We respect his memory and wish his soul safe journey.

Edwin Gerow
July 1973

Studies in the Language and Culture of South Asia

Two Indian Novels of Partition

Mano Majra and *Jhutha Sach*

Usha Nilsson

श्रीः For decades before 1947, Indians had looked forward to independence, hoping that it would bring the solution to India's myriad problems. Pre-Independence literature reflected this hope and the struggle for social betterment and desire of freedom from British rule. Partition came as an unexpected shock to millions of people. For many Sikhs, Hindus, and Muslims, it meant leaving familiar surroundings and moving to a new and strange part of the country, even when they were unwilling. In the wake of these mass uprootings came massacres, flamed by fanaticism and mostly from a blind, insane desire for revenge. Waves of hate engulfed all of North India, concentrating in Bengal and Punjab. The horror of partition and its consequences have been depicted in the two novels I discuss in this article.

Mano Majra,[1] also known as *Train to Pakistan,* is an Indo-Anglian novel of Khushwant Singh, a well-known writer both in India and abroad. Yashpal, on the other hand, is a veteran writer of Hindi, comparatively unknown in the West, except in Russia where several of his works, including *Jhutha Sach,*[2] have been translated. Both novels have won recognition. *Mano Majra,* a prize-winning novel, was chosen from among more than 250 entries submitted to Grove Press, New York, and *Jhutha Sach* has won awards from the states of Punjab and Uttar Pradesh in India. While *Mano Majra* has been called a contemporary historical novel in its finest sense,[3] *Jhutha Sach* is Yashpal's best novel so far and is easily one of the most significant in Hindi literature.[4]

There are several recognizable surface similarities between *Mano Majra* and *Jhutha Sach.* Both writers are deeply involved with the themes of human destiny at a time of national crisis, individual behavior under stress and pressure. Yashpal and Khushwant Singh have tried to interpret historical events: Khushwant Singh touches them briefly and only in the context of their direct bearing on action in the novel; Yashpal goes into greater detail because of his own political commitments and an involvement with history. Yashpal himself belonged to a group of young revolutionaries like Bhagat Singh and Azad in the thirties and spent part of his life in prison for his anti-British activities. He used his prison term for an extensive study of world literature and found himself attracted to Marxist doctrine. Though he never became an active Communist party member, his early novels show a strong leftist bias. This bias is not so apparent in *Jhutha Sach,* where he is trying to keep a very objective point of view. In the preface of an earlier novel he said emphatically that a writer should contribute to the development of a useful society, like any other worker.[5] In *Jhutha Sach* he aims to give a true picture of the social and political scene, tracing the factors that led to partition.

Both *Mano Majra* and *Jhutha Sach* could be called political novels. Irving Howe says: "By a political novel I mean a novel in which political ideas play a dominant role or in which political milieu is the dominant setting."[6] Joseph Blotner's definition is: "A political novel is taken to mean a book which directly describes, interprets or analyzes political phenomena."[7]

There is no doubt that both novels are deeply concerned with the phenomenon of a country dividing into two separate, political entities. The subject matters, the internal and external tensions of characters are born of this particular political milieu. Yashpal has used the methods of a political scientist in collecting data for his novel, so as to be absolutely correct in tracing historical events. He interviewed hundreds of refugees personally, carefully taking notes. He also spent several years reading the accounts of events occurring during 1947 and afterwards. Khushwant Singh has made use of general, rather than specific, facts that were known to most people in India and Pakistan.

But *Mano Majra* and *Jhutha Sach* cannot be called political novels only. They have considerable artistic merit and literary excellence; they are social and psychological novels as well. The dividing line in this case is very thin. Both novels are in a sense social documents rendering a traumatic experience. They depict the ambiguity of the partition, its negative and its positive effects on society. But Khushwant Singh selects only one aspect of partition, only one picture. He capitalizes on the most dramatic and horrifying events of the partition, the massacre of innocent men and women, homeward bound to India. He also takes up the problem of hate—Muslim hate for Hindus, Sikh hate for Muslims—and the fear from which it is bred.

Yashpal's *Jhutha Sach* is a saga of partition, running into two volumes of approximately twelve-hundred pages, covering all dimensions of life and a whole range of human experience. His choice of subject matter clearly reflects the vicissitudes of partition, as well as the emergence of national character from chaos and heartbreak. It gives an unusual glimpse of Indian life in all its multiplicity and variety. The story acquaints us with a representative section of life in contemporary India. The external action stretches from 1947 to 1957. Though its canvas is large, yet the novelist has entered the fine depths of life and in this way has provided both extensive and intensive study of the lives of the people involved in partition. The first volume deals with the humdrum lives of people in the city of Lahore, and the second shows many of these people in India as refugees and their efforts to put down roots in new soil.

Though Yashpal has depicted the lives of politicians, intellectuals, journalists, writers, social workers, businessmen, and just plain ordinary men and women, the focus of *Jhutha Sach* is the brother-sister pair, Jaidev and Tara Puri, two college-age children of a poverty-ridden schoolmaster. The first volume covers the story of Jaidev and Tara in their lower middle-class surroundings, all the people living in the same neighborhood—rituals, customs, fights, liaisons. Outside the narrowness of this social level they have a circle of friends at college, most of them coming from the better part of Lahore and from sophisticated families. We see Jaidev's political affiliations with the Communist party, his struggle to be self-supporting and also his growing love for Kanak Datta, daughter of a liberal, well-to-do publisher. Tara, Jaidev's nineteen-year-old sister, preparing for her B.A. exam, shares her brother's brilliance and his aspirations, though not his political allegiance. She is in love with a Muslim, Asad, an active worker of the Communist party. Tara is aware of political changes taking place in the country, but like many she is not overly concerned. Certainly she has no idea how these events are going to affect her. While her family pressures her to marry Somraj Sahni (a thoroughly undesirable character much below her intellectual level), she protests, rebels, asks her brother's help, and, failing on all sides, seeks out Asad to tell him she is prepared to elope with him. Asad's response stuns her. He says:

> I cannot do anything without the party's permission. It would be against the rules and in the present situation against common sense . . . at such a time before marriage and individual problems, come people and nation. We are all in danger. We can only think of ourselves after we cross these hurdles. . . .[8]

The rumblings of disturbances have been going on in Lahore for some months. In March the first death due to communal hatred occurs in Tara's neighborhood, riots are taking place and the anti- and pro-Pakistan groups are exerting their pressures. The young Hindu men of Bhola Pandeki Gali swear to take revenge for their Hindu neighbor's death. The communal war is on. The Muslims invade Hindu neighborhoods. They are met with a shower of bricks from the rooftops and with homemade bombs. The Muslim dead are dragged back to their own alley so as not to cause trouble with the police. The fate of Lahore and thousands of Hindus is undecided; some of the people have already started to leave. Summer comes and it is in the midst of the rioting, murders, and arson that Tara is quietly married off to the man chosen by her family. By now she knows the futility of hoping or waiting for Asad. The wedding night is a nightmare; her husband, who is aware that Tara was against the marriage, insults and beats her. At that point, their house is attacked by Muslims and set on fire. Tara escapes but the relief is momentary and towards the end of the first volume we find her in a refugee camp with many other abducted and homeless women. In the meantime, she has been caught by a Muslim and raped, tortured, starved, and pressured to accept Islam, which she refuses to do. Asad is one of the men helping the representatives of India to recover abducted women; he is shocked to find Tara in this camp and in this state. He tells her that she was thought to have died in the fire. He hesitatingly asks Tara what she would like to do—stressing that she can't stay in Lahore as long as she is a Hindu woman. But the decision is taken out of her hands when she is forced to leave the camp for India with the other women.

The second volume depicts the healing process, the refugee camps, the attempts of the government to rehabilitate the refugees, the murder of Gandhi, the political and economic changes, the social mores and the changed lives of Jaidev, Tara, Kanak, and many others. Tara has forsaken her family, against whom she is very bitter, because she knows that they will turn her over to her husband. She finds comfort in anonymity and lives with great courage and fortitude. Jaidev succeeds in marrying Kanak, becomes an editor of a progressive journal, and eventually enters politics as a member of the ruling Congress party. Though both Tara and Jaidev are successful in their new external lives, their personal lives have become empty and loveless. Eventually Kanak leaves Jaidev and obtains a divorce. Tara finds an older professor who knew her in Lahore and marries him. The novel ends on a comparatively cheerful note because Yashpal believes in the constantly changing power of people, their capacity to change their own and their country's destiny.

There are several other minor stories that run alongside the lives of Tara and Jaidev. One is of Tara's cousin Sheelo, her lover Ratan, and her husband Mohanlal; another is of Kanak's family; of her parents, sister, and her lawyer brother-in-law: all of these minor stories have a point of contact either with Tara or Jaidev's life. It is with the help of these concurrent narratives that Yashpal has been able to add variety and conflict on a larger scale. In the first volume the events leading to the partition play the dominant role; in the second volume the characters shape the events and their future.

It is through Jaidev-Kanak-Tara and their multiple and varied experiences that Yashpal has effectively conveyed the idea of a nation torn, millions uprooted. This family presents a microcosm of what happened to people during the partition.

The story of *Mano Majra* deals with the same kind of events that Yashpal has set out in the last seventy pages of *Jhutha Sach*'s first volume. Unlike *Jhutha Sach*'s broad and intensive treatment of political and human events, Khushwant Singh has been extremely selective. He does not trace the history of partition, it is an accepted fact when the novel opens. His main concern is to show how hate, fear, and violence enter into the lives of the unsophisticated people of *Mano Majra*, and how the dilemma of hate is resolved by unexpected courage and basic human goodness. He sets his story in the village of Mano Majra, at the Pakistan border. The villagers are unaware of the geographic and strategic importance of their village and are completely convinced that partition is not going to affect their lives. Mano Majra is by a river and the trains that pass over the bridge regularly set its clocklike routine. The rumors of atrocities being committed by different religious groups drift to Mano Majra, but do not disturb anyone, for Muslims and Sikhs have lived as friends for generations. Life goes on as usual. A young Muslim girl, Nooran, takes Jugga, a Sikh, for her lover; a government officer, Hukum Chand, is entertained nightly by a young Muslim dancing girl; a moneylender is killed by a group of robbers; the police investigations go on. But the time of grim realization comes for the people of Mano Majra when a train arrives carrying as its passengers the dead bodies of Hindus, coming into India.

> A soft breeze began to blow toward the village. It brought the smell of burning kerosene, then of wood. And then—a faint acrid smell of searing flesh.
>
> The village was stilled in a deathly silence. No one asked anyone else what the odor was. They all knew. They had known it all the time. The answer was implicit in the fact that the train had come from Pakistan.[9]

And with this ghost train comes fear, distrust, and foreshadowings of the storm. A sense of desolation comes to Mano Majra. People huddle together, ignoring their chores and wondering about their future. Another train carrying dead passengers arrives from Pakistan. The flooded river shows not the bodies of people who have drowned, but were murdered and then thrown in the river.

The atmosphere changes.

> Muslims sat and smoked in their houses . . . quite suddenly every Sikh in Mano Majra became a stranger with an evil intent. His long hair and beard appeared barbarous, his kirpan menacingly anti-Muslim. . . . The Sikhs were sullen and angry. Never trust a Mussulman; they said. . . .[10]

In this background the love story of Jugga, a Sikh bandit, and Nooran takes on added significance: Jugga stands not only for a Sikh lover, Nooran for not only a Muslim girl, but they also represent a microcosm in which love can surmount religious hatred or political discord. The second story, interlocking crucially with Jugga's, is that of Hukum Chand, who is a practical, hardhearted, government official; the youthful dancing girl, however, touches a vulnerable spot in his heart. A point comes in the story when law and order break down and communal feelings prevail over the sentiments of duty. Hukum Chand is very agitated to learn that the train going to Pakistan that very night is going to be ambushed, because the Sikhs want it to go full of Muslim corpses. At this sudden crisis Hukum Chand hatches a plan to release Jugga from the prison where he is being held on the false charge of murdering the village moneylender. The quick ending in the novel comes as the tension mounts and Jugga tries to cut down the rope barrier on the bridge while bullets ring around him. He is doing it for Nooran, who is also forced to leave the village of Mano Majra, and in one last sublime act he not only saves the girl who is carrying his child but hundreds of other innocent Muslim men, women, and children.

In this way *Mano Majra* is a sharp, poignant glimpse of partition and its tragic consequences, while *Jhutha Sach* is a detailed unfolding of history.

Though both novels use straight realism, one dramatically emphasizes the significance of the moral deed, while the other focuses upon psychological delineation of the characters.

While Khushwant Singh gives indirect, hearsay accounts of the atrocities, Yashpal gives direct, eyewitness descriptions of the murders and mutilation. In *Mano Majra*, the principal characters guess about the ghost train, but in *Jhutha Sach*, Jaidev is on such a train full of Muslims going to Pakistan. One lives through the stark horror when the train is stopped, attacked, women are dragged off and Jaidev and another Sikh escape only when they shout loudly that they are not Muslims. Khushwant Singh does not touch the refugee problem at all, but Yashpal has described in painstaking detail the destitution and utter hopelessness of people living in camps.

The action is illuminated in *Jhutha Sach*: it never dazzles, the writer moves at an unhurried pace. There is no climactic episode: the movement is like the rise and fall of sea waves. *Mano Majra*'s action moves very fast, so that one gets the impression that time is running out. The fast pace of action is one of the devices Khushwant Singh uses for crystalline effects.

While the characters of *Mano Majra* are sharply defined, *Jhutha Sach* builds them up brush stroke by brush stroke, very carefully and painstakingly. For this reason, in *Mano Majra* their latent attributes are suddenly revealed, in *Jhutha Sach* the reader has time to perceive the personality changes.

The helplessness of an ordinary man in the face of great historic change preoccupies both novelists. They both comment on the effect of social environments on people. Khushwant Singh in this respect has gone beyond the immediate and presents a key as to why the characters are what they are. Jugga's father was a criminal and he was hanged; it is obvious that Jugga is following his father's footsteps. It is a comment on society, which hasn't done anything to help Jugga to transcend his environment and have a fresh start. Jaidev Puri and Asad in *Jhutha Sach* are also unable to rise above their social environments. Jaidev, who has always encouraged Tara to study further and to develop her personality, lets her down when she needs his support most—to fight the family against an unwanted marriage. Asad, even seeing Tara in the refugee camp in all her misery, is unable to take a strong stand, he just hints that he is still interested.

Jaidev's weakness becomes more apparent later when he lets go of Urmila, a young widow who came to him after the partition and who was living with him, depending entirely on him for her brief spell of happiness. He is also unable to accept his wife Kanak's independence and emancipated outlook.

Jaidev has lived to conquer his economic difficulties, but he hasn't been able to rise above social pressures. Compared to men like Jaidev and Asad, Jugga in *Mano Majra* is strong, virile, and primitive. It is difficult to imagine that Asad would have sacrificed his life for Tara as Jugga did for Nooran. It could be that both Jaidev and Asad are crushed by their city living and middle-class subservience.

However, Khushwant Singh's characters, though successfully drawn, are stereotypes: Jugga is a typical delinquent; Hukum Chand, the typical government officer; Western-educated Iqbal is dissatisfied and ineffective; Bhai Meet Singh, platitudinous like most religious officers; the subinspector, a fumbling policeman who is not given any responsibility. An Indian reader recognizes them immediately as very ordinary people. Khushwant Singh's success lies not in the originality of characters but in their latent potential, which endows them with unique personalities as soon as they act out of the ordinary. Jugga, a bandit, is capable of an act of supreme sacrifice; Hukum Chand, the practical, cautious, scheming man, reveals a softer and better facet.

Yashpal's characters also come from real life, but they all possess strongly individual traits, and are blends of reality and imagination. Jaidev is not a typical Punjabi youth nor Tara an average Hindu girl. Not many girls have the initiative or the undaunted courage of Tara. Yet they both are realistic Indian characters.

Yashpal has used minor characters very effectively in *Jhutha Sach.* Enormous in number, they are instrumental in revealing the action unfolding on several levels simultaneously. They suffer and endure the ordeals of partition along with major characters. Some of them are necessary to give impetus to action at particular moments. Many of them are never heard or seen again. They are so realistically drawn as to make the reader often wonder through the second volume about their fate during the partition. They are the neighbors in Lahore, the Muslim families, Tara's friends in college, the abducted women. Though only one facet of them is seen, they are so convincing as to leave the impression of partition as a windstorm scattering leaves far and wide.[11] Sometimes they have not even a name or a face, just voices: a man trying to reason with the crowd when a Muslim girl is being held for auction; a woman chastising a Hindu family for not accepting a daughter-in-law who was abducted and tries to kill herself at her husband's doorstep; the innocent fruitseller; hill folk rejoicing in Naini Tal on Independence Day, not knowing the cost of Independence to many.

Then there are characters who, though secondary, play a very important role in the novel. Sister Mercy, Narottam, Sita, Puran Deyi, Tara's parents, her husband—all figure largely in the story and are revealed more fully—each has the potential of a major character, each contributes towards the progression of the narrative and successfully holds the reader's attention. In many instances these are the characters who provoke events with far-reaching consequences: for instance Tara's rich uncle and aunt who arrange her marriage and then pressure her parents to execute it in spite of Tara's protests. This action not only gives an unexpected turn to the story and directs Tara's future action, it also presents a very interesting study of interpersonal relationships and family loyalties in Indian society. In the same way, Mrs. Agarwala, in herself a very minor character, forces Tara to accept a job that opens the doors to professional success.

Khushwant Singh here is at a disadvantage because of the limited size of his novel. Even his major characters do not have scope for full development; his minor characters are just outlines, they are easily forgotten.

Mano Majra presents its women only as sex objects; Nooran and Hasina are young and beautiful and they accept their destiny as such. Yashpal includes women from different levels of society with different values. On top we have progressive and independent women like Dr. Shyama or Kanak; political and social workers, and Girja Bhabhi, who is respected in the Congress party and the town for her integrity and strong sense of moral virtue. We have a whole gamut of lower-class women, unsophisticated, but possessing native wisdom, mostly generous and helpful but mean and selfish on occasion. Bhagwanti, Kartaro, Meladai, Peeto, Pushpa, Basant Kaur are women living in the same cramped, middle-class neighborhood who get together to stitch Tara's trousseau, and yet pile curses and abuses on each other from their windows. Tara has grown up in this milieu, but her brother Jaidev's association has brought her into contact with girls from liberal families mixing freely with boys and generally regarding themselves as equal to men. Tara has imbibed their influence and she yearns for such a life. She has a strong personality and she is a fighter and a rebel.

On the wedding night she refuses to surrender to her husband who has taunted and insulted her, and who wants to have her just to establish his husbandly claim. Later the same night she fights physically; kicking, biting, and trying her best to ward off Nabbu, her Muslim abductor. She succumbs only when her strength gives out and she falls unconscious. This rebellious spirit is apparent when, homeless, she is living with a Muslim family and is rigorously pressured to accept Islam. She refuses firmly, not because she has any faith in the Hindu gods, but because Islam would not give her the answer she is seeking. Later, when she finds herself in captivity instead of a refugee camp as she was led to believe by the son of the Muslim family, she suggests to the women a way to get out. And once in a refugee camp Tara's life is a long, uphill struggle. She has undergone the worst of partition conditions and from this has acquired a deep humility, a sense of deterministic fate, and at the same time strength and courage. It is Tara who prevents her cousin Sheelo from killing herself in despair and gives her courage to go live with her lover Ratan, not caring about the conventional moral code. It is Tara who helps Sita rehabilitate herself instead of letting her become a woman of easy virtue. Tara has suffered a great deal at the hands of men: Asad leaves her in the lurch, her brother withdraws his support after finding that she loves a Muslim, her husband marries her to show his superiority, Nabbu not only rapes her but gives her a veneral disease. It is no surprise that she develops an aversion to males. Even when she finds her old benefactor, Professor Prannath, in Delhi as economic adviser to the Planning Commission, she is not prepared to marry him and when she does, once again she finds herself the target of her first husband's malice.

However, Tara can now successfully resist the pressure of society and help others to do the same. She emerges victorious in her struggle against misery and convention, and she is thoroughly convincing as the various incidents of her life give a fully believable motivation for her development from an inhibited, naïve, young girl to a strong, self-possessed woman. Tara is a skillful rendering of psychological realism.

Kanak shares the spotlight with Tara. Both are the products of the modern world, not only of New India. They have the courage to break the traditions, they have the strength to be independent, and when Kanak realizes that her marriage is dead, she leaves Jaidev instead of keeping up the age-old role of devoted wife. Kanak and Jaidev met and fell in love when they were young, but partition and reversal in family fortune helped Kanak to mature rapidly. She slowly becomes disillusioned with Jaidev who has compromised with life and suppresses the truth that Tara is alive in order to ward off an unpleasant situation with Tara's husband. Kanak also finds another man (Gill) and starts life anew.

The role that faceless, nameless people play in both the novels is significant. They constitute the crowds, the villagers, the inciters, the ghosts of the innocent dead, the floating population. It is one of them who starts the first fire, shoots the first round of bullets, stabs first, drags a woman out of the stopped train—and then hysteria prevails and there is no stopping. Their power is terrifying. They are secure in their anonymity. Interestingly, both Khushwant Singh and Yashpal seem to recognize that often the mischief was started not by ordinary, law-abiding people, but by persons belonging to a criminal fringe that always seems to be present in Indian society. Malli and his gang who were responsible for the Hindu moneylender's death loot the property of Muslims when they leave Mano Majra; Nabbu, a registered criminal, abducts Tara, steals her jewelry, and rapes her. It is such a business-minded, criminal type who starves the abducted women and, instead of turning them over to Indian authorities, sells them to men looking for wives in *Jhutha Sach.*

It is significant that both Khushwant Singh and Yashpal believe in the human power to decide if not all at least a few events in life. When the first wave of disturbances hits the characters, they are paralyzed, but then they struggle and get on their feet slowly. Hukum Chand is helpless at first, but then manages to save the train. In the first volume of *Jhutha Sach* the characters are not powerful enough to change the course of events. They are not entirely passive but power to make decisions is not given to them and they are victims of mass hysteria and the breakdown of law and order. They are freer to choose their destiny only after the events of partition, when the milieu has changed, old ties are broken, elaborate rituals are forgotten, people have undergone so much that they really can differentiate between what is important to them and what is not. Sheelo, spending an empty life with her husband and yearning for Ratan, consoled herself with the moral code proper for a traditional wife, but after the partition she is able to carve out a new and happy life with Ratan. Ratan's parents also overcome their reluctance and accept her as their daughter-in-law, because they are strangers in Delhi and no one knows that Sheelo is not their son's legal wife.

Khushwant Singh throws a little light on the contemporary political scene. In the course of conversation, both the subinspector and Iqbal blame the Congress party for its inefficiency and partisanship. Even the village folk think that freedom has given them nothing and that "We were better off under the British. At least there was security."[12] Yashpal, because of his political views, makes the partition setting a determinant factor for his novel. Starting with the demand for Pakistan on the part of the Muslim League, and its local and national consequences, he mentions major personalities of that time. His characters, especially in the second volume, discuss in detail Gandhi's stand on communal feelings, his fasts, Nehru at his most powerful, and underground Communist activities. He does not hesitate to have characters criticize Gandhi or Nehru or party politics in Punjab. On the other hand, he shows peacemakers on the ordinary level like the Railroad Workers' Union trying to prevent Hindu-Muslim killings in Lahore, the social workers busy in the refugee camps, the nobler souls trying to help. Iqbal represents the attempts of the People's party to maintain peace at partition in *Mano Majra,* but he comes out as nothing more than the square peg in a round hole.

Closely connected with Yashpal's political views is his treatment of the refugee problem. Even before the partition was accomplished, both India and Pakistan found themselves with thousands of refugees pouring in, and their care and rehabilitation was a heavy burden. This also revealed, on the human side, men and women sinking back to a primitive level. The women snarl and fight like animals for a piece of bread or some clothing, the refugee crowd is ready to lynch another refugee who has bought a house; the crowd wants to have a share. The moment a Muslim neighborhood is evacuated, refugees rush in to take possession. One of the major and insoluble problems is the abducted women whose parents or husbands refuse to take them back because according to the rigid Hindu code, they have been polluted by Muslim contact.

But not all refugees are alike. Many of the families start again, in adverse circumstances, and soon take over the economy of Delhi. Many of them are shown to be better off in India after a few years' independence than they were in Lahore. But Kanak's father who left his publishing business in Lahore finds there is no great demand for Urdu books in India.

Both authors have approached their material with a great objectivity and neither of them falls into the easy role of preacher. They regard themselves as social commentators, not moralists. On the other hand they make it clear that they have no faith or respect for the clergy, whether Hindu, Sikh, or Muslim, presenting them in a slightly ridiculous manner. Bhai Meet Singh is only a peasant who had taken to religion as an escape from work.

In *Jhutha Sach*, Hafiz Inayat Ali turns pious after he has led a life of cheating and deception. His entire concern for Tara's welfare is his hope of taking her into the fold of Islam and marrying her to some nice, righteous Muslim.

Both writers have leaned over backwards not to blame any one religious group for the disturbing events. Even when presenting the Indian side of partition they make it very clear that Muslims and Hindus and Sikhs share equal blame for atrocities. Khushwant Singh says in the opening chapter:

> Muslims said the Hindus had planned and started the killing. According to the Hindus, the Muslims were to blame. The fact is, both sides killed. Both shot and stabbed and speared and clubbed. Both tortured. Both raped.[13]

Written with convincing realism, Khushwant's treatment of the theme is still romantic and somewhat idealistic. This is apparent in the sudden metamorphoses of Hukum Chand and Jugga into men of great strength and heroism. Yashpal's tone is extremely impersonal, thereby lacking the flair of *Mano Majra*.

Both the novelists have used language with the controlled economy, facility, and force of experienced writers. They have effectively used irony and sarcasm. Khushwant Singh's English has overtones of Urdu and Punjabi, especially in conversation, which adds a distinctive charm to his diction. He has freely used the literal translations of Urdu vocatives, which sometimes carry different meanings for a native speaker of English. The use of "government" as a vocative to stand for "your honor" in English is a direct transplant from Urdu *Sarkār*, which carries both the meanings of "your honor" and "government."

The speaking voice of the author is very pronounced in *Mano Majra*. It is clear that Khushwant Singh is writing for Western readers and feels it necessary to blend explanatory passages with narrative, which an Indian reader finds not only unnecessary but irksome, for example, his homily on monsoons. At the same time Khushwant Singh has included a few elements that are clear only to an Indian reader, like his laughing at long South Indian names and hints of ethnic jokes.

Yashpal, writing for Indian readers, does not explain the vagaries of Indian weather or include explanations of rituals or customs that are an integral part of Indian life.

Tending to use a Sanskritized vocabulary in his other novels, Yashpal has discarded it in *Jhutha Sach* in favor of simple, clear, and effective Hindi. His diction is colorful with wide usage of different vernaculars. His educated characters, like most Indians, make frequent use of English words. The majority of his characters use understandable Khari boli, while women constantly use colloquial Punjabi. The meanings of these Punjabi vocatives, abuses, and endearments are given in parentheses to help a reader unfamiliar with their usage.

Yashpal's style is conservative, more literal than figurative. He is not eloquent, constantly gives an impression of understatement, thus passing up opportunities where he could have really moved the reader. His impersonal tone often prevents a reader from feeling with the character.

Since both novels are primarily social documents, it is natural that both authors have chosen the omniscient point of view—and let the various aspects of the subject come out through frequent shifts of the point of view.

Both novels can be called successful. Unfortunately the second volume of *Jhutha Sach* fails artistically as the author passes on to depict the emergence of a new and better order. He lapses from psychological credibility and vivid realism into a sociological, political essay in which the characters and their conflicts lose the earlier urgency and poignancy. However, both books offer an imaginative, well-integrated picture of a grave moment in Indian history and are significant contributions to Indian literature.

NOTES

1. Khushwant Singh, *Mano Majra* (New York: Grove Press, 1956).
2. Yashpal, *Jhutha Sach*, 2 vols. (Lucknow: Viplave Karyalaya, 1963).
3. Ibid., back cover.
4. Prakash Chandra Gupta, *Ājkā Hindī Sāhitya* (Delhi: National Publishing House, 1966), p. 138.
5. Yashpal, *Deshdrohi* (Lucknow: Viplave Karyalaya, 1961), p. 6.
6. Irving Howe, *Politics and the Novel* (New York: Meridian Books, 1957), p. 17.
7. Joseph L. Blotner, *The Political Novel* (New York: Doubleday and Co., Inc., 1955), p. 2.
8. *Jhutha Sach*, 1:228.
9. *Mano Majra*, p. 84.
10. Ibid., p. 121.
11. Prakash Chandra Gupta, *Ājkā Hindī Sāhitya*, p. 138.
12. *Mano Majra*, p. 49.
13. Ibid., p. 1.

Vaikom Muhammad Basheer

R. E. Asher

श्री: It has been observed by a number of commentators that speakers of any major Indian language will tend to be convinced that it is their literature that leads the field in modern India—a view that is above all, of course, the result of widespread ignorance of what is going on in other regions of the country.[1] This is just as true of the people of Kerala as of any other part of India, the only difference being, perhaps, that the Malayali enjoys greater success in persuading the outside observer that if one really wants to know something of the most flourishing contemporary Indian literature, one must make one's way to the southwest corner of the subcontinent.[2] Two conclusions are possible here: first, that the claim may be justified; second, that the Malayali is a better salesman. And it has to be stated firmly that no-one is in a position to judge between these alternatives. There is, however, no difficulty in establishing that Kerala's literature is in a very prosperous state.

One tends in modern times to judge a literature by the quality of its prose fiction, if only because this is the area in which the bulk of creative writing is to be found. Kerala is no exception and it is in the novel and the short story that the claim of Malayalam literature to have some sort of universal significance must be tested. The man whose writings I discuss in this paper seems unquestionably one of those demanding close attention in this context.

The history of prose writing in Malayalam follows the pattern common to almost every one of the living languages of India. Almost all the early literature is in verse.[3] There are inscriptions in prose, some possibly as early as the tenth century, and prose commentaries from perhaps the twelfth century onwards. Later come works falling more clearly within the field of literature, namely, the versions in Malayalam prose of Sanskrit *purāṇas*, which started to appear in about the fifteenth century. But it was only after European contacts had been firmly established through trading and missionary activities that prose began to be used really extensively.

The development of prose literature and printing have often been found, for fairly obvious reasons, to go hand in hand. The early establishment of printing presses in Kerala (by Jesuit priests) is therefore important here; the first press was set up in a seminary near Cochin in 1563 and two more followed within twenty years. In the early years more Tamil and Sanskrit were printed than Malayalam and, as is to be expected, the first books were almost without exception on religious topics. The early advent of printing in this region remains significant in the history of Malayalam.

Another important landmark was the production in the latter part of the eighteenth century of a book by a Malayali traveler giving an account in prose of a journey he made to Rome with a fellow countryman in 1778.[4] This book, by a local Christian convert, was the direct result of Portuguese missionary activity. Major developments in prose literature, however, came only after the establishment of British power in Kerala in the early part of the nineteenth century. The educational policy of the new rulers had a number of important effects. The need for the governed to learn the language of the rulers made many people aware of the salient features of European literature. In addition, the establishment of larger numbers of new schools, even if aimed ultimately at providing an English-style education, necessitated the production of new textbooks in Malayalam, and these were obviously written in prose. Widespread literacy followed these efforts in the realm of education at all levels and opened a market for the printed word. It is an anomaly that Malayalam, though having fewer speakers than most other major languages of India, is among the leaders in the number of books, newspapers, and magazines produced.

No discussion of the development of literary prose in a given language can ignore the date of publication of the first novel. Here Malayalam was not one of the leaders. Far ahead of the rest, of course, was Bengali. Malayalam's neighbour, Tamil, entered the field in 1879.[5] In the year after this a Malayalam translation of an English version of a Dutch novel appeared.[6] The first original novel, generally considered to have little literary merit, came out in 1887,[7] to be followed two years later by O. Chandu Menon's *Indulēkhā*,[8] a love story with a strong element of social comment and some political controversy, inspired by, though not based on, the author's reading of Benjamin Disraeli's *Henrietta Temple*. Chandu Menon and his slightly younger contemporary, the historical novelist C. V. Raman Pillai, have been described as the "only two giants" in the history of the novel in Malayalam.[9] This judgment, however, can probably be taken as a wish to avoid the controversy that would follow the inclusion of any living writer under the same heading. In spite of the great importance of *Indulēkhā* in the history of Malayalam literature, several better novels have been published during the last quarter of a century.

The work of these two great pioneers was followed by a period of relative stagnation, until a new flowering of the art of prose fiction in the thirties of this century. Much of the credit for this goes to a veteran critic and man of letters of the period, A. Balakrishna Pillai, who not only gave much encouragement to younger writers but also introduced them to the great nineteenth-century figures in the European novel and short story, including many, such as the French and the Russians, who were accessible only in English translation. Even now writers—and the reading public—in Kerala are quite exceptionally well informed about the European literary scene.[10] A remarkable number of extremely gifted writers, most of them born during the second decade of this century, were impressed both by what Balakrishna Pillai pointed their attention to and by his counsels to turn Malayalam literature in a new direction, away from romanticism and into realism. Many accepted his view that literature should be involved in social change and social progress. One might even trace the pan-Indian movement in favour of "progressive" literature to Kerala. Certainly it had an early beginning there.[11]

The leaders of the "realist" and "progressive" school had their earliest successes as short-story writers, but the best tended, as they developed their literary skills, to turn to the writing of novels also. Outside Kerala the best known is undoubtedly Thakazhi Sivasankara Pillai, than whose *Cemmīn* few contemporary novels have been more often translated.[12] Other outstanding novels have come from his very active pen, but they would seem to be too committed to a particular sociological point of view to find a ready publisher in the West. *Cemmīn*, that is to say, cannot be regarded as being at all typical of Thakazhi's work.

Vaikom Muhammad Basheer (Vaikkom Muhammad Baṣīr) has been grouped, along with Thakazhi, among the members of the "socialist realist school."[13] This classification is far less apt than in the case of others among his contemporaries, such as Thakazhi and P. Keshava Dev. Basheer, in fact, is essentially unclassifiable. It is true that his writing has an occasional element of social criticism, but this is implicit and never intrusive. Above all there is never the slightest hint of preaching. The story and, even more than this, the way of its telling are what count.

Basheer also differs from most of the others in not appearing to be subject to the same literary influences. Thus Thakazhi will state, and one can see this to be the case, that his work owes much to European writers such as Maupassant and Zola. Basheer, who has a profound knowledge of English and is very widely read, can point to no such influences.[14] He has no models, either admitted or discernible.

There is further difficulty in stating what sort of writer Basheer is, what the literary genres are of which he is a practitioner. Disregarding his one play[15] and occasional film scripts, since these represent untypical and nonrecurrent activities, one may say that his other writings belong to the field of prose narrative. But it is less easy in several instances to place them on one side or the other of the boundary dividing novel and short story. Basheer's own definition would appear to be that when he publishes one of his narratives as a book on its own (many will first have appeared in some periodical[16]), it is a novel, while a short story is a narrative that will come out as part of a collection appearing together in a single volume. Some of the shortest of the first group may, it is true, indicate a certain amount of classificatory hesitation, in that they come out bearing the legend "novelette" on the English false-title page commonly included in Malayalam books.

The question of length is but one aspect of the problem, and a trivial one at that. It is an exceptional Basheer "novel" that exceeds a hundred pages and only the most recent one even approaches two hundred.[17] The matter has received a good amount of attention from literary critics, even the best of whom like to classify the works they discuss. A. Balakrishna Pillai, in his introduction to *Sounds*,[18] which is a mere sixty pages long, argues that, in spite of its division into twelve chapters, this is not to be thought of as a short novel but as a long short story (the awkwardness of these antonyms is less felt in Malayalam, since the relevant term there is, so to speak "*small* story"). This has nothing to do with the number of pages, but is related to the technique of composition and above all to the "unity of impression" that is to be noticed here. *Childhood Friend* (82 pages),[19] on the other hand, says Balakrishna Pillai, is definitely a novel. M. P. Paul, whose contribution to literary criticism in Malayalam, in terms of quality, is unsurpassed, was less sure. For him this book lay on the borderline between the two.[20] It traces almost the whole life story of one of the two main characters and while doing so gives a most careful and detailed account of the personalities of those involved in the story. One can therefore justifiably call it a novel. Yet because it is but a short book and the author avoids digressions that might take attention away from the main theme, one might reasonably call it a short story. Clearly Malayalam could do with a word that would do the work done by *Novelle* and *nouvelle* in other languages.

One result of this feature of Basheer's work is that it is not realistic to discuss his "novels" and his "short stories" separately, though histories of literature, because of the virtual impossibility of writing them without some sort of pigeonholing, have had no choice but to attempt to do this.

Furthermore, it is not easy to speak of Basheer's work under the general heading of prose fiction (hence the choice, earlier in this essay, of the words "prose narrative"). Most of Basheer's books contain a considerable autobiographical element. The recognition of this, as with all writers of this type, does not mean that an awareness of the extent of the personal factor in a given story is relevant to an assessment of its literary and artistic merits. The works of few writers have been more of a "confession" than those of Goethe, with the result that they have held limitless fascination for the literary historian. Goethe's commanding place in the history of German literature nevertheless has nothing to do with this feature. The same holds true of a consideration of the worth of Basheer's work. Here, too, as with other aspects of his writing, there is a demarcation problem. When is Basheer writing fiction and when autobiography? A simple arbitrary decision is to say that what he publishes as a novel, "novelette," or short story is fiction, that is, needs to be assessed from the point of view of its success as a piece of independent creative writing. On the other hand, anything Basheer writes about himself in an introduction to one of his books can be taken as purely autobiographical. This cannot hide Basheer's creativity whenever he opens his mouth or takes up his pen. It is commonly said of a person that he must have led an exceptionally interesting life, when what is just as likely is that he has an unusual gift for making it seem interesting. The next best thing to reading one of his books is to listen to Basheer, a born storyteller, talk.

Occasionally a Basheer story will be planned while the events in real life on which it is to be based are actually taking place. An example is one of the best known of his short stories, "Birthday."[21] This is an account of one of the author's birthdays at a time when he was far from prosperous. Indeed the central theme is the question of how he can get a cup of tea. Though living in the cheapest lodgings he can find, he is behind with the rent, and does not have a single anna to his name. He does not even own the clothes he is wearing. Now, as he writes, the day is over and he is sitting under a solitary lamp on the edge of the backwater, where he has come with pen and paper because there is no oil in the lamp in his room. "I want to write my diary for the day from beginning to end. There is in it all the material for a fairly unusual short-story."[22]

Other stories may result from a more distant recollection of the events they relate, as in the case of *A Bhagavadgītā and Some Breasts.*[23] Three writers, the poet Changampuzha Krishna Pillai (a Hindu), the critic and novelist Joseph Mundassery (a Christian), and Basheer (a Muslim), once went to the house of one Nambudiripad, managing director of a publishing company that had most of the writers of the day under contract. Basheer begins by meditating on who could be considered the outstanding one among the three visitors, but then goes on to make clear the relationship—not immediately obvious—between the two parts of his title. It appears that Basheer used to get a complimentary copy of every book the company published and yet (on the grounds that a non-Hindu would not want it) did not receive a copy of an edition of the *Gītā* that they brought out, which somewhat peeved him, since it was quite an expensive publication. It happened that, while he was at the Nambudiripad's house an elephant went wild. It was decided to control it by building a wall of fire, and the necessary firewood was brought by a group of Nayar girls, who followed the traditional practice of not covering the upper part of their bodies when going to a Nambudiri house. The Muslim Basheer, after getting over his initial shock at seeing naked female breasts, took to wondering about the reasons for various social and moral conventions.

In both of these stories the happenings referred to are clearly factual. So are those in Basheer's most recent book, *The Magic Cat,* first published in 1967–68 in a Quilon weekly.[24] The animal that figures as the chief character is still to be seen as a member of the Basheer household in Beypore and it brought no small number of visitors to the house while its story was being serialised. One would not guess the cat's remarkable powers from its appearance. It is of average size, alert, slim, and athletic-looking. But none of this makes it unique. It was introduced to the family as a companion for Basheer's small daughter, who is also, therefore, one of the essential personalities in the story. The photographs and drawings that accompanied the original publication, however, do not appear in the book, and rightly so; for the value of the story does not depend on the reader's consciousness that it all really happened this way.

We are told that when it was born, this was but an ordinary cat. It was only later that certain remarkable things began to happen. As they happened, the possibility of an amusing and satirical novel presented itself to the author. For he was witnessing the *avatāra* of a magic cat in the shape of a by no means exceptional-looking pet. How else, for example, could one explain the sudden blossoming of a shrub that had never produced a flower until the cat came on the scene? Basheer has explained, in discussing the genesis of this novel, that there is a great readiness in his part of the world to believe in miracles. Attempts have been made to credit even him with divine powers, though his failure to convert the sand in the courtyard of his house to gold rather spoilt this image of him. Various episodes concerning the cat started him thinking about "the 'divinity' of Indian life." He notes that "The only surplus thing that India can boast of is our Gods and their divinity! New prophets and new incarnations appear all of a sudden in every nook and corner. And they vanish in the same way."[25] A little mild fun at the expense of false prophets seems very justified.

Frequently in Basheer's stories will be allusions to his profession as a writer. The direct reference in "Birthday" has already been noted. A feature of the saga of *Pāttummā's Goat* is the difficulty he experiences in getting the peace and quiet a writer needs in the noisy, overcrowded household, in which everything is made even worse by the appearance on the scene of an ubiquitous goat.[26] *Walls* mentions the writing he did while in jail.[27] A ghost story, "The Blue Light," finds him asking the spirit of a girl who committed suicide, supposedly residing in a house he has rented, not to disturb his writing.[28] In return he will let her have full use of half the house.

Not that there is a clear personal element in all of Basheer's works. Thus there is no reason to suppose that "Pūvanpaẓam," a sort of miniature *Taming of the Shrew*, is at all autobiographical.[29] "Pūvanpaẓam," one of the more delicious varieties of banana, is the symbol of the unreasonable demands of Jamil Beebi, Abdul Khadar's perhaps too well-educated wife, and of his eventual success in getting her to drop her attempts to change and "improve" him.

Sounds,[30] a more substantial work, is also "merely fiction," though a writer plays an important part in it. The story is that of a demobilised soldier, told in the first person. An abandoned child, he was brought up by a kindly foster parent until his adoptive father died. He was then in the army until the general demobilisation that followed the end of the Second World War. He recounts some of his wartime experiences, including the one that made the deepest impression on his mind—the request of a severely wounded comrade to help along his death. Now a civilian, he presents himself as a murderer. He tells, too, of incidents in his love life, among which is his relationship with a male prostitute, whom he had taken to be an attractive girl, and of contracting venereal diseases. He talks of the occasion when he saw a beggar woman leave her child crying on the ground while she went off with a lover. Eventually he became so disgusted with life that he tried to commit suicide by placing his head on a railway line, an attempt that failed because he miscalculated and chose the track adjacent to the one on which the train was about to pass. That the book accepts homosexuality as widespread and that it speaks of the contracting of syphilis and gonorrhoea have led to the quite unjustified assumption that it is a rather unsavoury book. Far from being pornographic, it is a searching examination of the nature of public and private morality and indeed of the whole meaning of life. It is concerned, too, with the futility of war and with the degradation of internal racial and communal strife. The sounds are both those that men try not to hear and those that formed the background to episodes in the soldier's life —the noise of battle, the shouting of slogans, the general din of the city. *Śabdaṅṅaḷ* are also the voices one hears on the way through life.

Not the least interesting aspect of the book is its form. It is cast as a conversation between the ex-soldier and a writer, a mere five years older than himself, whom he greatly admires and whom he visits unannounced very late one night. Comments and questions by the writer, who proposes to write down the soldier's tale, interrupt but do not disturb the latter's narrative. Only chapters nine to eleven (out of twelve) are made up of this narrative alone.

Superficially far less objectionable than *Sounds*, one of Basheer's novels, *Love Letter*, was nevertheless banned.[31] It was written in 1942, when Basheer was serving his sentence in the Trivandrum Central Jail, published in 1943, and seized and banned in Tranvancore in 1944. The book opens and closes with the text of a love letter written by Kēśavan Nāyar to Sāṟamma. When he takes the letter to her, she simply crumples it up and puts it aside. Conversation then turns to her problems. Though she has passed the Intermediate B.A. examination, she has found it entirely impossible to get work. Marriage seems out of the question also, for already three proposals that she received have fallen through because no dowry can be provided. On top of all this she is unhappy at home. Since her mother's death she has been looked after by her mother's younger sister. Now she finds herself blamed for everything, from her failure to obtain a husband to the weather. Kēśavan Nāyar's solution is to offer her a job himself. The work consists of loving him the way he loves her. Though she has expressed a willingness to accept any job at any salary, Sāṟamma hesitates for several days, ultimately agreeing, however, to take on this work for twenty rupees a month. At one point not long after this the young man's feelings lead him to attempt to kiss her, but he is told to keep at least four feet away, for this was not part of the contract.

Prodded by Sāṟamma, Kēśavan Nāyar applies for other posts and eventually obtains one away from home at a monthly salary of 250 rupees, which Sāṟamma interprets as meaning that her pay now goes up to 125! When Kēśavan Nāyar proposes that she come with him so that they can be man and wife, Sāṟamma points out the problems raised by their different religious backgrounds. Church and temple will always come between them. Even if they attempt a partial solution by having a registry-office marriage, children will bring further difficulties. What about a name for the child? He would not want a Christian name; she would object to a Hindu one. Yet a Muslim or a Parsee name would give a wrong impression about the child's religious adherence. A name from another source, such as a Chinese one, or a Russian one ending in *-ski*, would be impossible.

When the time comes for Kēśavan Nāyar to leave his home town to take up the new post, he packs his belongings with the feeling that Sāṟamma never in fact loved him. She has given no positive sign of it either by word or deed and now she is sending him away with no more than her blessing and an envelope that he has to swear not to open until the train is on its way. He hates all women. But she is there at the station when he goes for his train, having decided to join him. The envelope, he finds, contains all the money he has paid her as "wages." Moreover, his biggest surprise is that the love letter he thought was thrown away has been kept close to her heart through all the passing months.

The plot is thus not only a simple one, but one that could easily receive a "novelettish" treatment, in the pejorative sense of the word. Basheer's delicate touch, however, keeps it well away from this. In a sense the story is an examination of a social problem important in a society made up of as many different communities as Kerala's. There is, too, an implied attack on the dowry system still carefully adhered to by some sections of the population. Its more enduring and essential quality, however, is its skilful presentation, simple yet profound, of certain human emotions.

It is evident that, since no person in *Love Letter* is a Muslim, this work is among those that are not based on events in Basheer's own life. In the novels—the majority—that are in some sense autobiographical, the personal element shows in different ways and to differing degrees. As a general rule it can be assumed that if a story is told in the first person, then the "I" is Basheer himself. In one, quite exceptionally, he is addressed by another character as "Mr. Baṣīr." The reason, however, is quite trivial: a jailer switches to English to tell him "You can go Mr. Baṣīr; you are free!" The walls of this book's title are, as one would expect, those of the prison where he served a two-year sentence as a political prisoner.[32]

Basheer played a very active role in India's struggle for

independence and courted arrest for a long time, and one might anticipate that, since he himself figures so prominently in his books, this aspect of his life would play a big part in his writings. It is of course there, but never with a view to showing the heroic nature of the struggle or of Basheer's part in it. Nor is there any attempt to make anti-imperialist points. As always with Basheer, the story is more important than social or political comment. Thus there are references to his political activities in "Birthday," but only because at that time they had frequent repercussions, whether he sought this or not. So, as he goes around seeing various friends in the hope of getting a free cup of tea, he notices that a C.I.D. man is following him. Then, at seven o'clock:

> A policeman came to my place and took me along with him again. I was asked to sit before a dazzling petromax. As I answered the questions that were put to me, the Deputy Commissioner was walking up and down, carefully observing the expression on my face. . . . I was questioned for an hour: Who are my friends? Where do I get letters from? Am I not a member of a secret organisation which seeks to overthrow the Government? What new things have I been writing? I must tell the whole truth!
>
> "You know I have the power to exile you?"
>
> "I know. I am quite helpless. If a mere policeman takes it into his head he can arrest me and put me in the lock-up."[33]

And so, although he was allowed to go on this occasion, it eventually turned out, as *Walls* makes clear. Indeed he was held in the "lock-up" without trial for a year or more, and even then the case was only heard because he started kicking up a fuss and went on a hunger strike. *Walls*, however, is not about police brutality, nor about the harsh treatment meted out to political prisoners. "No-one beat me," he writes. "While in the lock-up I wrote a few police stories; the police inspector gave me pencil and paper."[34] Similarly, conditions in the jail could hardly be described as hard. The diet included hen eggs, he could drink tea, smoke beedis, read, and he learned how to play bridge. But the walls, towers, and doors remained, and everywhere were warders. Still, he got on well with the jailer and the prison superintendent and was allowed to cultivate a rose garden. All of this, however, as the opening sentence of the book makes clear, is merely the setting for a love story—and the strangest of all of Basheer's love stories—recollected in tranquillity years later.

The day he entered the jail his sense of smell told him there was a woman nearby, an impression shortly confirmed by a woman's laughter. For it happened that he was to be in a part of the jail that was adjacent to the women's prison. Eventually, despite the wall that separated them, they started to talk. He threw her a rose bush to plant on her side of the wall. She offered to cook something for him. Personal details were exchanged and after some time they arranged to meet in the joint prison hospital, planning carefully to ensure mutual recognition. Then, the day before the first possible time for a meeting, an order for his immediate release came through. So he was forced to turn his back on the walls that he had started by hating (especially when all the other sixteen political prisoners they enclosed were released), but had later begun to have different feelings about.

The quiet atmosphere of the jail is a far cry from the setting for the story of *Pāttummā's Goat.*[35] This is no less based on fact, and if no-one addresses Basheer by name here, it is merely because his position as eldest son demands respect. The story paints a remarkably convincing picture of the tumultuous nature of life in a large Muslim joint family. The family is Basheer's, all the book's characters are members of his family, and all the incidents it relates actually took place.

The family home is a small house and always overcrowded. Basheer therefore built a separate little house for himself alone, with everything that was required for peace and quiet. For ten or fifteen years, being in his younger years a great wanderer, he barely lived in it. This did not prevent him being extremely aggrieved when he came home with the intention of staying in it and found that one of his brothers had rented it out. He was just recovering from a spell of mental illness and needed tranquillity above all else. What he found, since he had to live in the main house, was perpetual din and disturbance. He lists the inhabitants of this small thatched building:

> There is my mother; my next younger brother Abdulkhādar, his wife Kuññanummā, their darling children Pāttukuṭṭi, Ārīpha and Subaida; the next brother after Abdulkhādar, Muhammad Hanipha, his wife Aiśōmma, their darling children Habība Muhammad, Lailā and Muhammad Ṟaṣīd; Hanipha's younger sister Ānumma, her husband Sulaimān, their darling child Saidumuhammad; and then my youngest brother Abūbakkar.
>
> So much for people. In addition to them are some cats that have come from somewhere or other to take refuge and live there under the protection of my mother; living in fear of these are hundreds of mice which are always scampering about in the roof-space. Cawing and kicking up a racket as they perch on the roof-top are the crows. Nor must one forget the hundred and one fowls which are my mother's own property and which are the rulers of the house. With them are chickens without number. In the trees are the hawks and kites which carry them off for food.
>
> The house is always filled with sound. . . . Children, cats, hens, women, kites, mice, crows—it's a real hullabaloo that they create together.
>
> Arriving in the middle of all this confusion, what do I see but a goat.[36]

The goat creates nothing but trouble. It goes everywhere, eats everything. It devours half of Habība's shorts when he challenges it to get a sweet from his pocket. It very happily puts away copies of Basheer's books *Childhood Friend* and *Sounds*. Its owner, Pāttummā, another sister, lives elsewhere with her family, but she is often at the house and the goat is always there. The goat's arrival results in more domestic quarrels than ever before, both among the children and among the adults—especially when she is seen to be in kid, for that raises the question of who should get the milk.

The sparkling narrative relates incident upon comic incident and in telling it Basheer makes lighthearted fun of every member of his family, including himself. Thus there was the time when he saw a number of schoolgirls talking together outside the gate of the house. He lay back in his chair and imagined the conversation they must be having about that "well-known literary man, Vaikkam Muhammad Baṣīr." They were obviously, he felt sure, just plucking up enough courage to come and ask him for his autograph. But when they entered the yard, they walked straight by him and up to his mother, whom they wanted to ask to sell them some fruit from the jambu tree. To make matters worse, it was *his* jambu tree.[37]

The picture of life at his home is not built up from incidents connected with the goat's activities alone. Many of these remind him of earlier events. Thus there are frequent flashbacks, especially to his own childhood, and it becomes clear that life in this family has not basically changed, except in the replacement of one generation of children by another—and in the fact that there is now a goat to keep stirring things up.

No two Basheer books bear a close resemblance, and one might say that no two are more different than *Pāttummā's Goat* and *Childhood Friend.*[38] They are alike in being mainly autobiographical. Basheer has said that "*Pāttummā's Goat* is a hundred percent my story" and that "*Bālyakālasakhi* is nearly ninety percent true to my life." But there the matter ends. It is not really the same sort of "truth." *Pāttummā's Goat* is filled with internal evidence that it is comprised of happenings in the author's life. We can only know that the story of *Childhood Friend* is largely Basheer's own story from his statement that it is. The story is told in the third person and the names are different from those of the real life characters.

Childhood Friend, which seems to be the author's favourite among all the books he has written, is a sad and touching love story, the story of Majīd and Suhrā. The opening paragraph elaborates on the title:

> Although Suhrā and Majīd have been friends since childhood, the one thing that is unusual about this

> affectionate relationship is that before they became acquainted they were bitter enemies. What was the reason for this enmity? They were neighbours; the families were on good terms. But Suhrā and Majīd were enemies. Suhrā was seven and Majīd nine.[39]

In these early days Majīd used to torment Suhrā in any way he could and was particularly careful to ensure that she never got a ripe mango as it fell from the tree near their house. She then learned to get her own back by scratching him with her sharp claws. But one day, in answer to an implied challenge, he climbed the tree, at the risk of being bitten by ants and having his flesh scratched by the branches, and plucked two fruits for her. So the relationship developed. Suhrā soon filled Majīd's daydreams, of the big and beautiful mansion he would own on the hilltop and in which she would be princess. At school she helped him with his arithmetic, for Majīd was bad at sums and obstinate with it too:

> Once the schoolmaster asked Majīd, "What do one and one make?" It is a fact well-known the world over that one and one make two. But when he heard Majīd's remarkable reply, the teacher burst out laughing. The whole class laughed. The reply he gave became his nickname. Before answering, Majīd reflected: just as two rivers join together and flow as one broader river, so two ones joined together become a broader "one"! Having calculated thus, he announced proudly:
>
> "A rather big one!"
>
> For finding a new theory in arithmetic Majīd was made to stand on the bench.
>
> "A rather big one!" They all looked at him and laughed. Majīd still didn't agree that one and one make two. So the teacher gave him six strokes of the cane on the palm of his hand and asked him to add all of them together and consider them as just one big one.[40]

The increasing closeness of their relationship is shown by Suhrā's anxiety when the time came for Majīd to be circumcised. This, as it happened, was closely followed by Suhrā's ear-piercing ceremony, which involved the making of eleven holes in the right ear and ten in the left. Though still confined to bed after his operation, Majīd got up and made his painful way to Suhrā's house for this event.

Suhrā's schooldays ended with the death of her father, for there was no longer any money to pay the expenses involved. Majīd got his mother to ask his father to pay for Suhrā. Father, a man of the most violent temper, refused. Did he not have sixty-seven dependents? Could he help an outsider and refuse them? Time passed by and a sort of sadness entered Suhrā's smile, as she had to shoulder the burden of supporting her mother and younger sister. Slowly the two childhood friends grew up until one day there came the realisation that "Suhrā loves Majīd; and Majīd Suhrā."[41]

Meanwhile Majīd was growing tired of the despotic manner in which his father ruled their household. One day things came to a head when Majīd forgot to run an errand he had promised to do. He was fiercely beaten and blows fell on his mother and on his two sisters also. Flung out of the house with the order to mend his ways, he felt he could stay no longer. So he went off, resisting the temptation to say goodbye to Suhrā.

> For seven years he travelled. Seven long years! During that time Majīd knew nothing of what happened at home or what changes took place in Suhrā's life. He sent no letters. Not because he didn't want to know: he didn't write, that's all. Suppose some-one came to look for him?[42]

Tired and dejected by what in the end seemed pointless travelling, he returned home "to marry Suhrā and spend his life somewhere quietly." But the changes that had taken place during his absence stunned him:

> All father's property has gone to pay off his debts. . . . Even the place they live in is mortgaged. His parents have become very old; his two sisters have grown up and passed the age when they should have been married. Above all, Suhrā is now a married woman! . . .

> It happened a year before Majīd's return! . . .
> Suhrā did not wait for Majīd.[43]

Majīd's mind became filled with two thoughts: the dreadful, destructive disease of poverty and his love for Suhrā. Not entirely by design the two met again and gradually it became apparent that essentially nothing was changed between them. Suhrā, it is true, had married, but only to avoid being a burden to others. Now she was extremely harshly treated by her husband. So she was often to be seen again in Majīd's parents' home and gossip started:

> For Majīd and Suhrā to talk to each other was immoral! Would not the sky break apart and fall!
> "What of it, if her husband kicked her once? When he beat her she might perhaps have lost a tooth! Still he's her husband!"[44]

Majīd's suggestion that he and Suhrā should marry was approved by his mother. But first his sisters must be married, and this meant he must find money for their dowries. Once again, therefore, though in a very different frame of mind, he left home. Getting money together from such work as he could find proved difficult and particularly so after he lost his right leg through falling off his cycle into some iron railings. After that the best job he could get, as dishwasher in a hotel, allowed him to save a mere five rupees a month. The vanity of all his efforts became clear when a letter from his mother informed him that the family property had been seized and the family evicted, and on top of this that their beloved Suhrā had died of consumption. "So our only friend and helper has gone."

In spite of the many light touches contained in the account of the childhood of the hero and heroine, this is clearly the saddest of Basheer's stories. It is not the sort of story that can stand any sort of wordy elaboration. So, as the extracts quoted will perhaps show, it is told in the simplest possible language and straight through from happy beginning to pitiful end. One can read into it criticism of Muslim customs, in particular the dowry system and the ceremonies of initiation for both boys and girls. as usual, it remains the story that really matters.

Basheer's most widely translated book, "*Me Grandad 'ad an Elephant!*,"[45] has a fair amount in common with *Childhood Friend.* It, too, is a love story of a Muslim couple, narrated in the third person, and inextricably mingled with the story is criticism of Muslim social customs, bigotry, and superstition. It is, however, autobiographical only in the sense that the personality of some of the main characters is based on certain people in real life, including Basheer himself. It differs also in being a more complex novel and can be read and enjoyed at several different levels. There is first of all the delightful and moving love story (with a happy ending this time) contained in the plot; there is an abundance of comedy; there is a fascinating presentation of the beliefs and practices of the old-fashioned Muslim; and there is the appeal to live in the present. Basheer has explained his intention in writing the book:

> My idea was to project the glory of the bygone days of Islam and at the same time to point out the failure of present day Muslims to adjust to the modern life because of this mythical past. Every beggar and every butcher even now claims that he is a direct descendant of Akbar the Great. The elephant is the symbol of that obvious past.[46]

Neither the elephant nor grandfather appears in the book. But the heroine Kuññupāttumma's mother is always talking about it. For her, her father's ownership of an elephant indicates that she belongs to a great family. So Kuññupāttumma must not talk to common Muslims and especially not to kaffirs.

When the book opens, Kuññupāttumma's father is well-to-do and a pillar of the community. Then he loses an expensive court action and falls on harder and harder times until in the end, like Majīd's family in *Childhood Friend,* he and his wife and daughter have to leave the family home. Past greatness, as symbolised by the elephant, is no help to them now. Worse than this, when the book ends, we see Kuññupāttumma's mother having to suffer the indignity of being teased by local children with the suggestion that this great elephant, known to all around, was not a real elephant (i.e., *āna*) but a mere *kuẓiyāna* (an "ant–lion," an insect whose diet is ants).

The descent from relative wealth to penury has a profound effect on Kuññupāttumma's life. Before a husband deemed worthy of her has been found, her father becomes too poor to provide a good dowry. In the meantime, Kuññupāttumma, who earlier entirely accepted the notion that a Muslim girl's duty was to accept without question the husband chosen for her, has met a well-educated young man who has bought the house next door (she herself is suitably ill-educated). Gradually the idea of marrying an unknown husband begins to be intolerable and she becomes extremely ill at the thought of it. The seeming impossibility of curing this "sickness" causes her parents unwillingly to draw back from their proposed course of action and a marriage is arranged with Nisār Ahmmad, the next-door neighbour, unorthodox Muslim though he is.

The various strands that go together to make up the book are indicated by carefully chosen chapter headings. The title of the book itself shows that we are concerned with the boastfulness of uneducated Muslims, for it is a dialect form of a sentence that would come out very differently from an educated mouth.[47] The book opens with the chapter, "This is a lucky mole!" As a girl, Kuññupāttumma was worried by the black mole on her cheek, worried, that is to say, until she learned why she had it. For was it not the same colour as her grandfather's elephant? Far from standing in the way of her getting a husband, therefore, it would help, since it showed what a fine family she came from. "Iblīs" (Satan) of the second chapter is the demon who sits on the shoulders of Muslims who do not follow correct and orthodox practices. Then comes the question, "Where Are the Kings and Others Who Boastfully Said 'I' . . . 'I?' As a prospective bride, Kuññupāttumma is examined not only for her appearance and whether, for instance, she has a full set of good teeth, but also for her knowledge of Islam. She must know about Allāh, the creator, about 'Ā'isha bint Abī Bakr, the Prophet's consort, about *al–Kiyāma*, the end of the world. On this day of judgment God Almighty will ask the question that forms the chapter heading. The "Two Old Wooden Sandals" of chapter 4 are a symbol of the class of Kuññupāttumma's mother. Not only does she always wear sandals, but their toe-pieces are made from ivory from the tusks of grand-father's elephant. So, even when they have to leave their big house, she is careful to take these old sandals along. The chapter that follows this is "The Wind Blew—the Leaf Did Not Fall!" The reference here is to "Sidrat al-Muntahā":

> It's in heaven. Sidrat al-Muntahā is the name of that huge tree. She Kuññupāttumma learned all this from the evening sermon she heard at the mosque. On the leaves of that tree are written the names of all living beings. When the wind blows, some of these leaves will fall. The beings whose names are written on these leaves will die. Of the leaves that fall, some are dry, some green and some tender.[48]

Kuññupāttumma's thoughts turn to this tree when her father in a fit of temper—extremely frequent now that life is so difficult—strikes her mother violently. She thinks he has killed her: but the leaf did not fall. In this way different episodes in the story bring in an account of various popular beliefs.

This chapter links up neatly with the next, "The Cry of a Sparrow." Kuññupāttumma is shocked one day to see two sparrows fighting. The loser (dead perhaps?) falls into a ditch. But its leaf, too, the small leaf of a female sparrow, has not fallen. She injures her arm getting into the ditch and as she struggles to climb out she finds Nisār Ahmmad staring at her. So the two meet and talk.

Later she meets the young man's sister, whom from her dress she supposed to be a kaffir and who calls her "Silly Ninny" because she is so backward and ignorant. So Āyiṣa starts to teach Kuññupāttumma educated ways of speech. But Kuññupāttumma's mother is not impressed by these neighbours:

> "They are not Muslims! It is I, the dear daughter of Ānamakkār, who tell you—they are not Muslims!". . .
>
> "Do you see the signs that *al-Kiyama* is coming?"
>
> Āyiṣa and her father and mother are signs that the world is coming to an end!
>
> "Look, that woman has flowers on her hair . . . flowers!"

> Āyiṣa wears flowers on her hair. Is that proper for a Muslim?
>
> "And did you ever see such a sight as that girl. She has done her hair in two plaits and brings them in front of her shoulders!"[49]

Thus easily is an old-fashioned person shocked. And so the story progresses to the final chapter, "The New Generation Is Talking": the new generation, which has no respect for those who live in the past, the new generation as represented by the urchins in the street for whom there was no elephant, merely an insect.

This book is a masterpiece—a point, however, that can only be demonstrated by careful and detailed reference to the text. Without this, one is forced to fall back on such familiar clichés as the one that says that it is impossible to change a single word without spoiling the book. It is this factor, among others, that makes the book so difficult to translate. In a restricted sense the meaning of any single paragraph can be given in acceptable English, but the construction of the whole work is so skilful and so intricate that one rarely has the choice of a number of synonyms for a given vocabulary item in the original. Each part of the book is full of subtle allusions to what has gone before and what follows. There will be frequent echoes, occasionally with slight but deliberate distortions, of earlier phrases. Similar care is taken with the intertwining of the various strands—sentimental love story, humour, social criticism, presentation of Muslim beliefs, and practices—that run through the book, so that they cannot be seen as separate strands. Essential, too, is Basheer's refusal to use two words where one will do equally well.

Though it can be argued that the literary merits of "*Me Grandad 'ad an Elephant*!" are not open to question, the book came under attack from a number of quarters. One motivation for the criticism seems to have been a fear that the author might make too much money. Basheer has described the way in which the book became a weapon in the hands of politicians:[50]

> As soon as it came out in book form, two remarkable things happened. One, the Congress Government gave me some five hundred rupees, saying that it was the

> best novel of those years. (Don't misunderstand this. It was not the Congress Government of Kerala, but of Madras.) The second remarkable thing was that the Communist party criticised the book unmercifully, saying that it was against the Communist ideals. . . .

The book continued to have success as a piece of literature:

> [It] was awarded the M.P. Paul Prize. After that the book was selected by the Centre Sahitya Akademi to be translated into fourteen or eighteen Indian languages.

There was, however, a change in its political status:

> The Communist party came to power in Kerala. Whether to my good fortune or bad, "*Me Grandad 'ad an Elephant!*" was prescribed as one of the texts for non-detailed study. (After the revered Parasuraman created Kerala, this is the first such incident. That is to say an incident when a Muslim's book was accepted at least as a non-detailed text. As it was the Communist Government that did it, this must be taken a little bit seriously. Conveniently forget, therefore, all the other books that were accepted and oppose this one.) So opposition started. . . . Everybody opposed it—the Catholic Congress, P.S.P., Congress, Muslim League. If what I saw in the papers is true, they all told plenty of lies about it. I am an old Congressman. I have taken a lot of beatings and punches and gone to jail several times. When I hear of Congress I think of Mahatma Gandhi, Indian independence and the like. Congress, which is supposed to represent non-violence and truth, need not have stooped so low. . . . [Yet] the opposition [in the legislature] made me a Communist party member.

Opposition or not, the book continued to sell and will no doubt go on doing so for a long time. The features that distinguish it as a work of art are no mere accident. To his inborn skill as a storyteller Basheer adds an enormous amount of hard work. Once written, a book will be revised in Flaubertian fashion until it satisfies the author's exacting literary standards. In this Basheer differs much from his equally distinguished contemporary, Thakazhi, whose *Cemmīn,* for example, is said to have been written in three weeks,[51] and who is a prolific writer. There are, however, occasional exceptions to the rule that the published version of a Basheer novel will differ considerably from the story as first written, as Basheer himself has stated in his introduction to *Pāttummā's Goat*:

> I completed the story *Pāttummā's Goat* on 27 April, 1954. I thought I would copy it out and publish it with an introduction. Days went by as I kept putting it off till tomorrow.
>
> Five years passed!
>
> Till now I have not copied the story. Almost all that I have published before this I have written and rewritten more than once. This is coming out without being copied, without any corrections, just as I wrote it. I read it through and did not feel that it should be corrected or copied.[52]

This judgment would seem to be the right one, for *Pāttummā's Goat* is a "fun" book that would not benefit from the careful polishing that Basheer normally gives to anything he publishes. It is the sort of book that needs a spontaneity that careful and painstaking revision might conceivably have removed.

None will quarrel with Basheer's description of *Pāttummā's Goat* as a gay book. This, however is the dominant, not the only mood. One of the justifications for regarding Basheer as a "realist," is the way in which his books represent one of the simple facts of life—that life is never entirely gay nor entirely serious. The serious side of *Pāttummā's Goat* is the recognition that the women of the family, unmerciful though the teasing he subjects them to may sometimes seem, merit admiration for the way they scrimp and scrape to make ends meet and the way they make sacrifices so that the children may eat well. *Childhood Friend* is a sad tale, but there is no lack of fun and humour, especially in the scenes of childhood. It is a dismal story that the soldier tells in *Sounds*, but he is able to see the irony of the situation when the "girl" he falls for turns out to be a man, or when his suicide scheme misfires.

Though usually extremely meticulous about preparing his writings for the press, Basheer is far from being a pedant. In this lack of interest in what a normative grammarian might consider "correct" style and usage, it is perhaps significant in the broader context of the development of Malayalam prose that he resembles other important Malayalam novelists and short-story writers who in other respects differ considerably from him. Thakazhi, for instance, will claim that he "knows no grammar," that is, he could not recite rules from a grammar book. Kerala's first outstanding novelist, Chandu Menon, belonged to the same school of thought. He chose to write his *Indulēkhā* in the language he "would ordinarily speak at home,"[53] avoiding Sanskrit words, for example, except where they would occur in normal, everyday conversation.

There is, however, more to Basheer's prose style than a simple adaptation of modern colloquial forms. Dialect forms, as is usual in contemporary prose fiction in Malayalam, are used in conversational parts of his stories when some useful artistic purpose will be served. More importantly, the prose of the narrative sections is also varied to suit the type of story. A recent book, indeed, matches the narrative to the dialogue. *Tārā Specials* is the story of the castles in the air built by Pāppaccan, who thought to make a little quick money by setting up a cigarette factory, named after Tārā, his bride-to-be.[54] The success of the project depends on his getting some financial help from a rather better-off lawyer friend, Pōḷi, and, more particularly, on his somehow obtaining a cigarette-making machine that he supposes their very rich mutual friend, Prēmraghu, to have. The whole project falls through when it turns out that this machine is the ordinary type used for making individual cigarettes and worth about ten rupees. This is a world of get-rich-quick, not overly scrupulous (they are not averse to a little smuggling), hard-drinking, chain-smoking young men. Their conversation is filled with repeated catch phrases and a heavy admixture of English vocabulary,[55] a fact that is reflected by the narration, the style of which is nevertheless skilfully differentiated from the conversational parts of the book.

Though, as has been seen from examples referred to, Basheer writes about members of all the major communities in Kerala, his attention is most commonly directed to his own Muslim community; and though it is not always easy to balance the diverse merits of one of his books against another, one might say further that his best stories are those with a Muslim setting. Paradoxically it is perhaps those books, which clearly mark the author as a Muslim (no-one but a Muslim could ever have written *Pāttummā* or the *Elephant*, for example), that have the most universal appeal, not only to non-Muslims in Kerala, but also to readers elsewhere in India and, given the chance, other parts of the world. This and the quality of being endlessly rereadable, may be what enables one to suppose that his books may become "classics."

NOTES

1. On this point see K. M. George, "Malayalam," in *The Novel in Modern India*, ed. Iqbal Bakhtiyar (Bombay: The P.E.N. All-India Centre, 1964), p. 81.

2. Cf. John Ashmead, "Indian Writers and Writing," in Program for *Festival from India*, Philharmonic Hall, Lincoln Center for the Performing Arts, July 25 to July 31, 1966: "From a writer's point of view, the most interesting of all the Indian regional languages is that of Malayalam in the southern state of Kerala" (p. 24).

3. On the origins and development of prose literature in Malayalam, see P. K. Parameswaran Nair, *History of Malayalam Literature*, translated from the Malayalam by E. M. J. Venniyoor (New Delhi: Sahitya Akademi, 1967 [Malayalam ed., 1958]), pp. 79–85, 115–21; and K. M. George, *A Survey of Malayalam Literature* (Bombay: Asia Publishing House, 1968), pp. 126–34.

4. Pāṟēmmākkal Tōmmā Kattanār, *Varttamānappustakam*. See Parameswaran Nair, *History of Malayalam Literature*, pp. 84–85, and K. M. George, *Survey*, p. 132.

5. See R. E. Asher, "The Tamil Renaissance and the Beginnings of the Tamil Novel," *Journal of the Royal Asiatic Society*, 1969, pp. 13–28.

6. Kērala Varmma, *Akbar*. See Parameswaran Nair, *History of Malayalam Literature*, p. 118.

7. T. M. Appuneṭuṅṅāṭi, *Kundalata*. See Parameswaran Nair, *History of Malayalam Literature*, p. 122, and Verghese Ittiavire, *Social Novels*

in Malayalam (Bangalore: The Christian Institute for the Study of Religion and Society, 1968), pp. 3–4.

8. Oyyārattu Cantu Mēnōn, *Indulēkhā. Imgliṣ nōval mātiriyil eẓutappeṭṭiṭṭuḷḷa oru kathā* (Kōẓikkōṭu: Spectator Press, 1889). An English translation by W. Dumergue was published by Addison & Co., Madras, in the following year (reprint by Mathrubhumi, Calicut, 1965). For an account of the content and nature of this novel see R. E. Asher, "Three Novelists of Kerala," in *The Novel in India: Its Birth and Development*, ed. T. W. Clark (London: Allen & Unwin, 1970), pp. 208–17, and Krishna Chaitanya, *A History of Malayalam Literature* (New Delhi: Orient Longman, 1971), pp. 260–66.

In the body of this paper, authors' names are consistently cited without diacritics in an anglicised form used by the writers themselves when writing in English. A simple roman transliteration of the Malayalam names would be (in order of appearance): Vaikkam Muhammad Baṣīr, O. Cantu Mēnōn, C. V. Rāman Piḷḷa, A. Bālakṛṣṇa Piḷḷa, Thakaẓi Sivaśaṅkara Piḷḷa, P. Kēśava Dēv, M. P. Pōḷ, Caṅṅampuẓa Kṛṣṇa Piḷḷa, Jōsaph Muṇṭaśśēri, Nampūtirippāṭu, K. M. Jōrjj, P. K. Paramēśvaran Nāyar, E. M. J. Veṇṇiyūr. In footnotes, when Malayalam works are referred to, the author's name appears in the transliterated form. Malayali authors of works in English, however, appear in the spelling chosen by the author for the publication of the work in question.

9. See K. M. George, "Malayalam," p. 84, and *Survey*, p. 174.

10. A not untypical example of this interest in European literature is contained in A. Balakrishna Pillai's introduction to Basheer's *Śabdaṅṅaḷ* (first published 1947), in which he refers to the work of Rimbaud (and Enid Starkie's study of the poet), Kipling, Jacobs, Katherine Mansfield, H. G. Wells, Tolstoy, Gogol, Maupassant, Somerset Maugham, Petronius, Diderot, Balzac, Goethe, Flaubert, Lamartine, Verlaine, Pierre Louis, Thomas Mann, Swinburne, D. H. Lawrence, H. E. Bates, Remarque, Zola, and, from India, Tagore and Mulk Raj Anand. Nor is this mere name-dropping.

11. See Parameswaran Nair, *History of Malayalam Literature*, pp. 260–61.

12. *Cemmīn* [Shrimps] (Kōṭṭayam: Sahitya Pravarthaka Co-operative Society Ltd.—hereafter cited as SPCS, 1956). English translation by Narayana Menon under the title *Chemmeen* (London: Gollancz; New York: Harper, 1962).

13. E.g., by K. M. George, "Malayalam," p. 87, and *Survey*, p. 177.

14. On this subject, both in general and these and other writers in particular, see K. M. George, *Western Influence on Malayalam Language and Literature* (New Delhi: Sahitya Akademi, 1972), pp. 89–113.

15. *Kathābhījam* [The Seed of a Story], included by Parameswaran Nair as one of a group of "significant additions to the problem play" (*History of Malayalam Literature*, p. 161).

16. Though in several of the other languages of India a number of

novels appeared in serial form before the end of the 19th century, Basheer would seem to be one of the first writers in Malayalam to serialise his work. See K.M. George, *Survey*, p. 186, and Parameswaran Nair, *History of Malayalam Literature*, p. 146.

17. *Māntrikappūcca* [The Magic Cat] (Trichur: Mangalodayam, 1968). 182 pp. of text. Before this the longest had been "*Nṟuppuppākkorānēṉṯārnnu!*" ["Me Grandad 'Ad an Elephant!"], new ed. (Kōṭṭayam: SPCS, 1961), 115 pp. and *Pāttummāyuṭe āṭu* [Pattumma's Goat], 3rd imp. (Kōṭṭayam: SPCS, 1962), 101 pp.

18. *Śabdaṅṅaḷ*, 5th imp. (Kōṭṭayam: SPCS, 1963). 1st ed. 1947. See Introduction, p. 7.

19. *Bālyakālasakhi*, 13th imp. (Kōṭṭayam: SPCS, 1961). 1st ed. 1944.

20. See the Introduction to *Bālyakālasakhi*, pp. 6–7. This assessment of the book is reproduced from Paul's *Nōvalsāhityam*. See reprint of revised edition (Kōṭṭayam: SPCS, 1963), pp. 275–79.

21. "Janmadinam," in the collection of stories of the same name, 4th imp. (Trichur: Mangalodayam, 1957), pp. 1–25. 1st ed. 1944. The author's English translation of this story is included in *Contemporary Indian Short Stories*, Series II, ed. Bhabani Bhattacharya (New Delhi: Sahitya Akademi, 1967), pp. 137–46.

22. "Birthday," English translation, p. 138.

23. *Oru bhagavadgītayum kuṟe mulakaḷum* (Kōṭṭayam: SPCS, 1967).

24. *Māntrikappūcca.*

25. Personal communication.

26. *Pāttummāyuṭe āṭu*, 3rd imp. (Kōṭṭayam: SPCS, 1962). 1st ed. 1959.

27. *Matilukaḷ*, 2nd imp. (Trichur: Current Books, 1967). 1st ed. 1965.

28. "Nīlaveḷiccam." In *Pāvappeṭṭavaruṭe vēśya* [Poor Men's Prostitute], 4th imp. (Kōṭṭayam: SPCS, 1964), pp. 7–26. 1st. ed. 1952.

29. In *Viḍḍhikaḷuṭe svarggam* [Fools' Paradise], 5th imp. (Kōṭṭayam: SPCS, 1963), pp. 20–41. K. M. George's *Survey of Malayalam Literature* contains appendices giving contemporary poems and short stories in translation and includes an English version of this story, under the title "Poovan pazham" (pp. 269–80).

30. See above, notes 10 and 18.

31. *Prēmalēkhanam*, 6th imp. (Trichur: Current Books, 1963). 1st ed. 1943.

32. See above, note 27.

33. "Birthday," English translation, pp. 145–46. See above, note 21.

34. *Matilukaḷ* (1967), pp. 7–8.

35. *Pāttummāyuṭe āṭu* (1962).

36. Ibid., pp. 25–26.

37. Ibid., pp. 60–63.

38. *Bālyakālasakhi*. See above, note 19.

39. Ibid., p. 9.

40. Ibid., pp. 26–27.

41. Ibid., p. 53.

42. Ibid., p. 57.

43. Ibid., p. 58.

44. Ibid., p. 74.

45. "*Nṟuppuppākkorānēṇṭārnnu!*" (1961).

46. Personal communication.

47. I.e., instead of *nṟuppuppākkorānēṇṭārnnu* one would get something that could be approximately symbolised by *enṟe uppuppākku orāna uṇṭāyirunnu.* (These transcriptions have no purpose other than suggesting the extent of the difference between the two forms.)

48. "*Nṟuppuppākkorānēṇṭārnnu!*" (1961), p. 53.

49. Ibid., p. 84.

50. *Pāttummāyuṭe āṭu* (1962), Introduction, pp. 7–10.

51. See Narayana Menon, "Thakazhi Sivasankara Pillai," *Indian Literature* 5, no. 2 (1962):14–20.

52. *Pāttummāyuṭe āṭu* (1962), Introduction, p. 11. It is worthy of note that, while the forthcoming 5th impression of this work is virtually unchanged from the 1st, the forthcoming 16th impression of *Bālyakālasakhi* is an extensively revised edition of the text of the 15th, with an entirely rewritten final chapter.

53. *Indulekha* (Dumergue translation, 1890), p. vi.

54. *Tārā speṣyals* (Trichur: Mangalodayam, 1968).

55. On one page alone are the following English words (over half of them in the narration): present, whisky, silk, shaving set, soap, Made in England, hip-pocket, blade, shave, razor, stainless steel, guarantee, fit, rolled-gold frame, style, rubber band, zig-zag (ibid., p. 66). The whole effect is not unlike that of Etiemble's *Parlez-vous franglais?* (Paris: Gallimard, 1964).

Alienation in the Modern Hindi Short Story

Gordon C. Roadarmel

> Men look at each other with suspicious and fearful glances, and having put the blame upon others, look away. They fear to meet and day by day grow more unacquainted and more distant with each other. The one seated in the chair and the one standing on the footpath both feel themselves to be useless and alien . . . knowing that no train will come, and that all of life will be spent waiting on the platform.[1]

श्रीः

This is the way one young Hindi author describes the world in which today's Indian writers are living, the world that provides the context for many of their stories. That author, Rājendra Yādav, goes on to point out that the literary result of this feeling about life, of this state of mind, is that the stories being written today in Hindi are "largely ones of breaking relationships—of people growing more and more alone and estranged—distrusting or hating the older generation—and unacquainted amongst themselves."[2]

Such a state of mind is certainly familiar to Western readers, reflecting some of the central concerns in Western literature and society. However universal the experience of alienation, though, its nature is likely to vary in differing societies. This study will attempt to identify some of the particular preoccupations in the modern Hindi short story since Independence, hoping thereby to locate some of the tensions in the urban middle-class Indian society on which these stories focus.

About 120 stories by 19 authors have provided the basis for this study, special attention having been given to a group of writers who attained prominence in the nineteen-fifties by writing what came to be known as *nayī kahānī*, the "new story." These authors now range in age from thirty to forty-five. A younger generation has since emerged that generally rejects the *nayī kahānī* writers; but there is no clear picture as yet of the nature of the very latest short fiction. This study therefore looks at the writers who, in the fifties and early sixties, made the short story the central genre in Hindi literature today, a position challenged only by Hindi poetry.

By the early fifties, the "progressive movement" in Hindi literature had almost died out. A younger generation, uncommitted and disillusioned, was appearing, concentrating primarily on the short story. Generally these writers held no strong faith in particular ideologies, being disappointed with Soviet and Chinese communism and disillusioned with the democratic capitalism of the West.

The new literature largely ignored both political and major social issues, focusing instead on a much smaller world of the family, of interpersonal relationships, and of the individual cut off from larger social groupings. *Nayī kahānī* stressed an experimental approach, searching for new literary forms and for a more realistic approach to human problems. The authors felt that earlier writers had tended to give easy answers to the problems of the individual and of society. These new writers were concerned to present the problems of existence without proposing solutions for them. They claimed to reject all conventional values, not only those of Marx or of Gandhi. One writer declared that "such scraps of useless convention as humanism, patriotism, leadership, truth and pride in the past are impractical, unscientific and reactionary." [3] In fact, though, the literature was usually not as revolutionary nor as lacking in traditional ideals as writers and critics declared.

Nayī kahānī writers identify a modern consciousness as one that deals with the immediate environment, largely ignoring the past and the future. Their stories include few historical or rural settings. Few stories deal effectively with upper-class or lower-class life. The world of the story is primarily the middle-class urban world of the Hindi writer himself. Authenticity is seen as lying in personal experience, and the result seems to be that a whole generation of writers is now concentrating on the individual rather than looking at life or at some formula of life.[4] And within the individual, the state of personal unhappiness appears to receive the most attention.

The world of *nayī kahānī*, however, is rarely a world of total meaninglessness. The complete outsider with no sense of loss or guilt is seldom depicted. More common is a strong sense of defeat or helplessness, implying some nostalgia for a life preceding or apart from estrangement and alienation.

The term "alienation" describes a variety of experiences or states of mind that are prominent in the contemporary Hindi short story, provided that the term is used in its broadest sense to include the various areas of personal and social experience in which an individual becomes cut off or feels himself cut off from others, from society, from religious or social institutions, or from himself. Alienation then covers a variety of related feelings—of isolation, estrangement, disaffection, indifference, disillusion, and loneliness.

A full analysis is impossible of the body of literature dealt with in this study, but a summary of some findings can be reported in four areas: alienation in the family; alienation in marriage relationships; wealth, status, and the urban setting as factors in alienation; and alienation for the person alone. Some attention will then be given to the over-all picture of Indian society suggested by these stories.

Alienation in the Family

In the traditional Hindu family, one of the primary sources of security for the individual was the joint family system. In the urban setting of *nayī kahānī*, it is not the joint family but the primary family—parents and children—that is depicted. Those primary relationships obviously become more crucial when an individual is removed from the context of support provided by the extended family or by the caste; and writers frequently take up the question of what happens to a person when even primary family relationships begin to disintegrate.

A conspicuous feature of short stories dealing with parent-child alienation is that sympathy is least likely to be directed to the father. In father-child conflicts, the father is almost always presented as the one at fault. In the depiction of mother-child conflicts, on the other hand, the child is usually pictured as the one at fault, rather than the mother.

A number of stories show fathers who are primarily victims of circumstances, a target more for pity than for blame. Another common character is the withdrawn, unapproachable, unaffectionate father. Often writers portray the father who is not only weak or aloof but immoral or tyrannical. In such cases, the most common response of the son is to leave home in righteous protest. Clearly the image of the good father is one who keeps himself above all suspicion of loose conduct, which reflects on family honor and is intolerable for a child. Significantly, these stories seldom show a son questioning the rightness of his indignation or trying to understand his father's point of view. Something happens, one person slams the door, and that is more or less final.

Open rebellion against a father appears clearly to be a valid or even an heroic option. Such rebellion against a mother is almost never depicted. Alienation between mothers and sons usually is seen as taking place after sons have met the family expectations, having married well and obtained good jobs. Now they are bigshots and indifferent to their parents, especially their mothers. The mother's response is usually one of long-suffering. She is usually anxious to avoid initiating any conflict, though her submissiveness may then be a major factor in sustaining misunderstandings and alienation. The general impression in these stories seems to be that any open expression of grievances should be repressed. The suffering parent or the suffering child puts up with the situation as long as possible and then seeks physical escape, rather than trying to reach a solution by confrontation.

The Hindi stories generally idealize the mother figure. She takes the child's side against an oppressive father, though usually fruitlessly. She tries to hold the family together. Where unsuccessful, it is because she cannot negate the pressure of a dominant father or because she is not in a position to protest a child's selfish indifference. There are some indications that the taboo on showing a "bad mother" is breaking down among younger writers, and occasionally a very unpleasant mother is depicted, but she is senile or insane, so not to blame.[5] Another story told in the first person denounces a mother; but the attack is so violent and unreasonable that the reader presumably realizes that the son is really at fault.[6] The next step would obviously be the depiction of a mother directly responsible for family conflict and alienation, a depiction that is practically nonexistent in the *nayī kahāniyān.*

A few stories deal with a generational gap, as in Gyānranjan's "Śeṣ hote hue" (Coming to an End). An older brother returning to the family home discovers that the other children have set up independent rooms within the home and that they entertain in their own rooms. "This is only the beginning," thinks the brother, realizing that the whole framework of the family is collapsing. Close, dependent, family relationships are the ideal.

In these stories of family conflict, the expectations for the family seem to be quite traditional: the father to be moral, tolerant, loving, and approachable; the mother to stand up for the children, to be morally blameless, loving, and long-suffering; the children to show affection and concern. Any deviation from these expectations is seen as leading to alienation and estrangement.

Family members are seen as very sensitive to any behavior or attitude in others that could be interpreted as slighting to themselves. They seem less sensitive to the ways in which their own behavior and attitudes might cause offense. So when a situation of tension arises, the response is usually to leave home or to remain in a state of passive suffering. People are depicted as quick to assign blame and to slam the door on the one at fault.

Given such an explosive combination, one might expect family alienation to be inevitable. But one also sees a strong, commonly shared acceptance of family roles, and a strong conviction that close family ties are crucial. The alternative, to move away from the family, is not pictured as likely to offer the prospect of happiness. One is not likely to find an alternative, in love or in meaningful work, to family security. No one wants to be alone, and to break with parents or with offspring is seen as leading to aloneness.

Alienation in Marriage Relationships

The largest factor leading to conflict and alienation in marriage relationships in these stories is the system of arranged marriage, which brings together two strangers on the basis of parental selection and expects them to spend their lives together. The stories do not suggest that this is a poor system or that marriages by self-choice would be preferable. The characters generally accept this social pattern, but many stories bring out the resulting difficulties. Marital conflict here is not so much alienation in a love relationship as estrangement between two people brought together by circumstances.

Few stories show children actively protesting an arranged marriage. Marriage may be entered with serious reservations or regrets, but, once accomplished, the partners attempt to make the best of the situation. The authors concentrate more on difficulties after marriage than on resistance to it. And if the selection turns out to be unsatisfactory, recrimination against the parents is almost never expressed. There appears to be a deep-rooted acceptance of marriage as a permanent institution not subject to dissolution. Family and social pressures also help couples to establish a working relationship. No nostalgia is seen for the joint family system, which is more likely to be shown as a hindrance to a young couple.

Most of the unhappy couples in these stories are childless, and are also separated from their families. In such circumstances, two people are naturally most dependent on each other, and incompatibility would produce the greatest strain. When there are children, the personal happiness of husband and wife seems to be less important. Wives especially are expected to find fulfillment in their children more than in their husbands. Stories about the childless wife stress not the difficulty of her social position, but the personal emptiness that results when there is no strong relationship with the husband.

In a society with strong taboos against promiscuity, sex could be expected to serve as a strong bond in marriage. Since sexual relationships begin from the point of view of strangers, however, rather than of lovers, sex is often shown reflecting incompatibility rather than promoting intimacy. In most of the stories of alienation between husbands and wives, there has been no love at any time in the marriage and sex is then seen primarily as an unsatisfying symptom of estrangement.

Although male authors predominate, the focus in these stories is more often on the wife than on the husband. She is the one to be pitied. The writers appear to sympathize with a wife who looks elsewhere for some affection if the husband does not provide sufficient love, but any deviation from complete fidelity, however provoked, is considered inexcusable by husbands in the stories. Even knowledge of a mildly affectionate relationship before marriage is likely to lead to disaster. There is no question of a wife justifying any type of infidelity to her husband, nor does one see husbands stopping to consider in such cases whether they might be partially at fault.

A wife is primarily expected to be absolutely faithful. Secondarily, she is expected to be submissive. A few stories, though, show the problems of wives who have these traditional virtues but are married to modern men who want a more outgoing, independent, and educated companion. Especially in lower-class families, the wives are pictured as submissive and long-suffering, expecting no more than some affection and some understanding from their husbands. Perhaps the reader's sympathy is usually with the wife because she expects so little, and her husband demands so much—not great love, but all the qualities in a wife that one would ask of an obedient servant or slave.

In situations of tension or conflict, withdrawal and silence are the most common response. When partners do try to discuss matters, little seems to be accomplished. As in the stories dealing with parent-child conflict, there is seldom any attempt to find out what the other person is feeling or to project one's self into the other person's situation.

Most of these stories suggest that there is little solution to the tensions in a strained marriage and almost all end with equal or greater alienation, rather than with resolution. Little hope of happiness is offered by breaking up a marriage. Occasionally a couple is seen as separating, but almost inevitably the result is continued, and often heightened, unhappiness.

The women in these stories generally expect to find their total satisfaction within the family. Few have occupational or intellectual interests that could provide another dimension of meaning to life. The men are shown as somewhat less dependent on marriage and the family for satisfaction, but a man who has left his wife like a man who has left his parents, is usually pictured as lonely and miserable.

The initial cause of alienation in many marriages, then is that two strangers are put together and are never able to establish any bond of affection or of compatibility. The gap widens in the absence of understanding and communication. When tensions develop, a lack of love, humor, insight, and of other interests aggravates the situation. So a few couples separate, but the rest resign themselves to a life of suffering or to a relationship of indifference.

Few characters in these stories know how to deal with disillusion in a marriage partner. They have had little previous experience in affectionate relations with the opposite sex, so their reactions to disappointment often have the naïveté of a first unhappy love affair. Unfortunately there appears to be small chance to try again and it is not surprising that when one wife hears the sound of a wedding band in the distance—"in the silence of the enveloping night, it sounded like someone weeping."[7]

Wealth, Status, and the Urban Setting as Factors in Alienation

Alienation in family or in marriage relationships appears to be especially threatening because there is so little sense of community beyond the family in the urban middle-class settings of most of these stories. There is no caste or village community to provide support; an individual cut off from family is largely on his own. The way in which others treat him appears to depend largely on the status he has acquired, primarily through wealth.

The authors seldom refer to caste status, and alienation from the caste community is not an important concern in the stories. Alienation is more often seen as a function of class, with people of higher status ignoring, mistreating, and being estranged from those of lower status. The higher class is cut off from the middle class, and the middle class from the lower class, the distinctions being wealth and occupation.

Wealth is generally looked on with suspicion. The stories suggest that wealth breeds indifference and contempt for others, that high status leads to a reduction of fellow-feeling. Typically, in Bhīsham Sahnī's "Kuch Aur Sāl" (A Few More Years), the man of wealth and status finds that he is expected to preserve a distance from his employees and from the public. That distance begins to extend to his own family, and the man ends up alienated from his own human feelings, living alone with a desk full of bills and accounts but no personal letters, rereading old newspapers, playing solitaire.

The greatest sympathy is directed to those at the bottom of the social scale. In Shekhar Joshī's "Dājyū," a lonely village boy is working in a city cafe. A customer, new to the city and also lonely, recognizes the child's accent and name and is delighted to find that they come from neighboring villages in the hills. The child showers the man with affection, calling him *Dājyū*, "big brother." Once the man feels at home in the city, however, he resents the boy's familiarity and shouts, "Don't you respect anyone's status?" The child, crushed, goes home that day with a headache. Some time later another customer asks the boy his name. Lest the man place him and repeat the pattern, the child responds only: "They call me Boy."

A similar situation is developed in Mohan Rākesh's "Mavālī"; an urchin in Bombay with no status or connections is wrongly accused of stealing from a family he has tried to befriend. The story ends with the boy standing on the beach cursing the waves.

The writers, themselves primarily of the middle class, often focus their stories either on the sterile life of people who are high on the social scale or on the broken spirit of people who are at the bottom. When looking at the middle class in the urban setting, stories frequently show the loneliness and alienation that comes from moving into a city. Many characters in the stories, like many of the writers, are from a smaller town and seem unprepared for the discovery that the city is a different world, where relationships have to be developed on a new basis, apart from traditional family or community ties.

The narrator in Kamleshwar's "Khoī Huī Diśāen" (Lost Directions) has moved to Delhi from Allahabad three years before, and is working as a writer. Typically, he expresses no satisfaction in his job or in his business contacts. The story reflects his feelings of alienation as he wanders around the city during one day. "Hundreds of people were passing by, but no one recognized him." In Allahabad, there would be a flash of recognition even when strangers passed; but in Delhi, the streets seem to lead nowhere, houses are protected by gates, there are warnings to beware of dogs, and one has to ring doorbells and wait.

The narrator makes a few attempts to break the isolation. He takes a ride in a scooter-cab whose driver he recognizes; but the man only asks for more money at the end of the trip. He goes to see an old girl friend, now married, but feels like a stranger when she doesn't remember how much sugar he takes in his tea. The alienation from himself is evident throughout:

> He'd not even had time to talk to himself; . . . He smiled slightly and made a note for each ensuing Friday—I have to meet myself from 7 to 9 p.m. And it was Friday today. This very day the meeting should take place. He looked at his watch—it was 7 o'clock. But why not have a cup of tea at the teahouse instead? Somehow he became disturbed at the thought of meeting himself.

The basic problem for this character is a familiar one in the *nayī kahānī* literature: a lack of inner resources that leads to a need for reassurance and support from outside sources. The fault is not that of the city, but life in the city aggravates the condition.

The story ends with the man retreating to the familiarity of his home and his wife. He seeks escape in sexual relations, but afterwards feels abandoned, "like a shell washed up on an unknown shore." When the wife goes to sleep, he is again tormented by loneliness and meaninglessness; and the story concludes with his waking her and asking, "Do you recognize me? Do you know me?"

As in most of the stories, it is clear that this character's alienation is far from complete. He suffers acutely from a sense of not belonging, but that suffering indicates that he still feels a strong need for human contacts. He is not estranged from basic human values, but cries out against the impersonality of the city.

A number of stories show people in the city being treated as commodities. Factory owners are indifferent toward the condition of workers; a man reluctantly attends a funeral and then is pleased at the excuse to take a day off from work; people are harassed by bureaucracy. Again, there are few solutions, except as some characters are able to stand out against the forces of indifference and inhumanity. A factory worker after some time is still conscious of the stench of oil on his hands, where the other workers no longer notice it.[8] In Dūdhnāth Singh's "Pratiśodh" (Revenge), a man and his wife are defeated in their battle with a company that owes them money. The man's revenge is that he accepts defeat, finding that through defeat he at last shares a common bond with the other people of the city.

Many stories of loneliness and alienation in the city present characters who appear to be having their first experience of being alone, of homesickness. Lacking training for independence, they feel lost and helpless, like children discovering for the first time that outside the home they can't count on the same automatic love and concern they found within the home.

The ideal society, one would gather, would have the characteristics of a huge family or of a giant mother, enfolding him with love just because he exists and regardless of what he does. To have to win people's affection is not a common expectation. As a result, the city reflected in these stories is a place where many people need and expect love and understanding, but few people give it. One story pictures the consequences: "the streets and sidewalks are crowded, but each person, wrapped in fog, seems like a drifting ghost."[9]

Alienation for the Person Alone

As already suggested, most of the stories indicate that meaningfulness in life depends heavily upon the presence, the physical closeness, of other people. To be alone is a great threat. The *nayī kahānī* authors rarely suggest ways of overcoming loneliness; they portray the feelings of people who are alone. Rarely do such characters have any meaningful interaction with society; rarely are they able to establish new relationships. Aloneness and the consequent loneliness are seen as forces that stunt emotional growth, pushing people farther and farther away from the possibilities of happiness.

Few characters have deliberately or voluntarily chosen to live alone. Separation from one's community or family is almost always portrayed as the result of pressing circumstances. A man usually goes alone to the city for studies or in search of a job, or occasionally to escape an oppressive family situation. The woman most often leaves home to become a teacher—ordinarily only a job would justify a woman's living by herself.

Men alone in the city tend to assume that marriage is the one way to resolve their loneliness, that any woman would be better than none. Since the man finds difficulty in arranging a marriage by himself, he is likely to eye—or to phantasize about—the woman next door. For women alone, marriage is usually not seen as likely and there is instead a retreat to some memory of love or of a time when she felt needed. The woman alone often lives in a world of the past, unable to establish new relationships.

The characters of these stories, both men and women, seldom have any interest in work, in ideas, in art, in culture, in social groups, or in politics. Their world narrows to their own rooms, and because no one shares those rooms they are desolate. They often talk of themselves as ghosts, feeling that life has ended: resignation and a desire for escape are more common throughout this literature than resistance or a willingness to struggle.

The person alone is characteristically unable to analyze his own situation, to see alternatives or to resolve his unhappy position. He seldom looks inward to ask why aloneness necessarily produces loneliness or estrangement. The authors are very concerned with *what* their characters feel, but are relatively unconcerned with the question of *why* they feel that way. Where a character does find some resolution to the problem of alienation through aloneness, it usually comes through some assurance from outside, not by discovering inner resources or an appreciation of independence.

In general, then, the person alone and threatened with a loss of identity in these stories feels little personal responsibility for his unhappiness. Self-reliance is not an expected virtue. The character awaits love and acceptance. Without it, he retreats further into self-pity. Perhaps surprisingly, there is little contemplation of suicide, little alcoholism, little antisocial behavior. Most of the characters are shown keeping up a respectable front to the world. But the man alone seems to have little hope that he can make friends. Either he is in a position to command the respect and attention of others, or he is ignored.

The extent to which such a body of literature can be used as a basis for generalizing about Indian society is very debatable.

The writers have chosen a small area of focus, and this study deals with only a part of that area. Conclusions from the literature need to be checked against observations made by scholars investigating other aspects of Indian life. Nevertheless, one can make some suggestions about the picture that emerges.

It would seem that to avoid alienation, one needs either some strong group support, as could come through family, caste, or community, or he needs a strong sense of self, of individuality. Traditional Indian society has provided strong family and community relationships. There is some indication that little stress was put on the development of a strong sense of self-worth or of individual identity. Dependence rather than self-reliance is expected of women and of young people generally.

Thrown into an urban setting, cut off from traditional family and group support, a person might well experience the kind of helplessness that appears in these stories. The response of the person alone is not "What can I do?" but "What is to become of me?" He might find strength in psychological insight into himself and others, in a capacity for independent thought, or in a willingness to accept responsibility for himself. But for many characters in these stories, there is little in their backgrounds to prepare them for solitude or for self-reliance.

A decline of social and political idealism has perhaps aggravated the situation depicted by contemporary writers. Earlier writers could feel that a return to traditional values, or independence from economic and political bondage, would restore wholeness to life. The modern writer, though, is skeptical of religious beliefs, critical of social customs, disillusioned by economic and political systems. The authors and their characters have not yet grown used to the resultant pain, and they dwell most strongly on their intense feelings of unhappiness. But few stories suggest that one cannot expect life to make sense. The world of the individual is still seen in the context of a meaningful universe where one should be able to find love and security. The alienated state of mind may be depicted as common, but not as inevitable; there is still a desire to restore the sense of belonging.

At present, the characters in the dominant stories reflect a strong self-centeredness. Few are shown making strenuous exertions for the sake of others. Efforts are largely aimed at satisfying one's own immediate wishes and desires. The apparent inability to improve life leads to helplessness and despair. Perhaps this kind of alienation can be seen as productive in the long run, however. Undoubtedly there will be increasing urbanization in Indian society, and a further breakup of the joint family and of community loyalties. The need would then be to develop greater individual strength and greater individual responsibility. The struggle against estrangement is likely to be painful, but, it is hoped, could lead to the development of new types of social relationships, which could support those cut off from traditional values and family ties.

Young people raised in an urban environment will perhaps prepare themselves earlier to be self-reliant, and feel less threatened by relative isolation. Thrown on their own, some people will inevitably flounder, and these people predominate in the present literature. Others, though, could in time be expected to develop by necessity greater insight into themselves and into the nature of urban life—where automatic acceptance cannot be expected, and where greater effort is needed to find affection and to win respect on the basis of one's own personality, efforts, and achievements. Increasing exposure to strangers could perhaps develop a greater ability to establish meaningful relationships outside of the traditional categories. And a greater sense of dedication to work or to social causes might provide a way to break the isolation, to relate one's self to society.

It seems likely however that, as in the West, Hindi literature and Indian society will continue to confront more and more directly the possibilities of meaninglessness. There is no easy way to resolve a sense that

> Men look at each other with suspicious and fearful glances, and having put the blame upon others, look away. They fear to meet and day by day grow more unacquainted and more distant with each other. The one seated in the chair and the one standing on the footpath both feel themselves to be useless and alien . . . knowing that no train will come, and that all of life will be spent waiting on the platform.

NOTES

1. Rājendra Yādav, *Ek Duniyā: Samānātar* (Delhi: Akshar Prakashan), 1966, p. 21.
2. Ibid., p. 31.
3. Ibid., p. 24.
4. Nāmwar Singh, *Kahānī: Nayī Kahānī* (Allahabad: Lokbharati Prakashan, 1966), p. 223.
5. Dūdhnāth Singh, "Raktpāt."
6. Gyānranjan, "Sambandh."
7. Rāmkumār, "Kitnā Samay."
8. Shekar Joshī, "Badbū."
9. Kamleshwar, "Dilli Meṇ Ek Maut."

[Ed. note: Some needed details are lacking in these notes; the manuscript was in this form at the time of the author's death.]

Faith and Love in Bengali Poetry

Edward Dimock

श्रीः When I was thinking about this paper, I asked several of my colleagues, people from different parts of the Indian subcontinent, how they would define the relationship of faith and belief, and whether they had different words for the two in their respective languages. The answers were generally what was expected. One of my more thoughtful friends, however, a man from South India, cocked his head and in true Hassidic manner told me the following story:

> A childless woman went to a famous rabbi and said to him, "Rabbi, I have only this pittance and this single piece of cloth; accept them and give me your blessing, that I might bear a child." The rabbi blessed the woman, and in time she bore a fine son. Another woman, hearing of this occurrence, went to the rabbi and also offered him her few coins and last piece of cloth, in return for the blessing that would gain her a child. But the rabbi said, "But this will not work for you, because you have heard the story."

The point of this story cannot really be understood if one considers it in terms of what the word "belief" comes later to mean—as Tillich says, "the acceptance of statements without evidence." The woman in the Hassidic story certainly has faith that what happened to the other woman could happen to her also.

Her condition however is not right; and faith itself is not efficacious.

If we take the notion that faith is love and that this is the first step toward union or reconciliation, we might also consider the notion that the proper vehicle for the expression of love is poetry in its true form, a personal and necessarily oblique attempt to try to express the inexpressible. This is perhaps most easily seen in the Vaiṣṇava sect of Bengal, which not only held this position but tried to describe it systematically. But it is discernible in traditions closer to home. The Persian Sufi poet writes of his Beloved, whose long tresses, often hiding her face, are dark as night, whose lips are rubies, whose body is the cypress tree in the nightingaled garden, whose eyes are pools to drown in. And St. John of the cross hears his soul, the Bride, sing:

> There in my festive breast
> walled for his pleasure-garden, his alone,
> the lover remained at rest
> and I gave all I own,
> gave all, in air from cedars softly blown.[1]

And the great troubadour Bernard de Ventadour, somewhat more bluntly, sings:

> If only she were bold enough
> to lead me one night, there,
> and naked take me in her arms . . .[2]

And later on, of course, Donne (especially in *The Extasie*), Crashaw, right down to Gerard Manley Hopkins and Coventry Patmore. The point at the moment is not the erotic imagery in the religious context, although that has its interests from several points of view. It is that although the imagery speaks of union, the poetry is essentially a poetry of separation, a love poetry of man's longing for his original and true state of belief. It is in a sense unthinkable that Hafiz or St. John or even the overt Bernard were considering actual sexual union with the deity, or the Christ. The primary characteristic of any devotional religion is dualism; if it were not, as the Vaiṣṇavas are quick to point out, one ends up worshiping one's self. The love of man for God, and the poetic expression of this, must use the erotic image, for the range of analogy in human experience is limited. And, as the Vaiṣṇavas say, separation is as much a necessary part of the love condition as is union; for if there were no separation, there could be no dynamic coming together—no reconciliation, to use the Christian term. The separation part of the love image is a statement of the human condition. The union part of the love image is not on this level of analysis, in orthodox Vaiṣṇavism at least, more than a metaphor suggesting the ultimate end of man—perpetual worship and devotion, giving pleasure thereby to the deity and gaining increased pleasure in return.

Let us look at one or two Vaiṣṇava lyrics to see how this duality is expressed; it will be possible to move from this to the detailed statementof how the Vaiṣṇavas describe the relationship of faith to belief. There are two general statements that must, however, be made first. The first is that these lyrics are immediate and spontaneous expression of *bhakti,* or devotion. The theological texts attempt to justify this spontaneous expression, just as texts of esthetics justify poetry by analyzing what makes it good or bad. The second is that there are some conventional symbols running throughout the poetry that must be understood. They are not unfamiliar, except in terms of explicit terminology, and the very familiarity lends weight to arguments about the sameness of devotional religions.

In the first place, the story that the poems describe or illustrate is the love story of Rādhā and Kṛṣṇa as it is told in the tenth book of the *Bhāgavata purāṇa,* a text of the ninth or tenth centuries, probably from south India, and in later texts such as the twelfth century *Gītagovinda* of Jayadeva. As a matter of fact, Rādhā as a character does not appear at all in the Bhāgavata story, though there is mention of a special girl among the Gopīs, the cowherd girls of Vṛndāvana with whom Kṛṣṇa carried on his amours. But she soon develops into the symbol of the soul of man, with Kṛṣṇa both the cowherd boy, enchanting in his beauty and object of the desires of the Gopīs, and the great god whose loveplay with the Gopīs is both *līlā*—love sport unexplainable to the human mind—and didactic. For, as the ultimate in attractiveness, Kṛṣṇa causes the Gopīs to leave their homes, their families, their honor, and come to him in the forest in the night. This is the proper attitude of the devotee, prepared to give up everything for his love and longing for God. Further, the descriptions of the love affair between Kṛṣṇa and the Gopīs or Kṛṣṇa and Rādhā show all the characteristics of a complicated human love affair: the initial infatuation and fright, attraction and dislike, pique and passion, separation and union, until finally Kṛṣṇa leaves the fields of Vṛndāvana, with the Gopīs grieving, in order—and it is stated—that by their longing and their grief their true love for him will grow. Let us look at the poems.

As water to sea-creatures
  moon-nectar to *cakora* birds,
  companionable dark to the stars—
my love is to Kṛṣṇa.

My body hungers for his
  as mirror image hungers
  for twin of flesh.
His life cuts into my life
  as the stain of the moon's rabbit
  engraves the moon.

As if a day when no sun came up
  and no color came to the earth—
that's how it is in my heart when he goes away.

Vidyāpati says, Cherish such love
and keep it young, fortunate girl.[3]

Two of the images of the poem are primarily conventional. First of all, the poetic conceit is that the moon is full of nectar; and *cakora* birds are those fictitious creatures who are said to live on moonbeams. And secondly, the stain on the moon, the "man in the moon" as we call it, is in the Indian convention a rabbit or a deer. And along these lines, traditional metaphors of the beauty of the beloved's face is the moon: "her face is like the moon," or, more appropriately here, "the moon seems stained, when put beside her face," which is flawless.

Structurally, the poem itself is a fine piece of work. On the most obvious level, the poet presents us with a progression from the darkness of the sea, the darkness of the night made darker by the stars, through the brightness of the mirror, the pure light of the moon, with emphasis on its purity, or the purity of the face of the beloved, through mention of the stain; and finally, in the fourth verse, he contrasts this progression from darkness to light, from loneliness to sexual union (note the use of such words as "engrave" and "cut" in the third verse), with the even more desolate loneliness that Rādhā feels at Kṛṣṇa's departure.

The poem as a poem, as a love poem, seems to me a gem. But the poem must also be read as a religious poem, though we might not know it if we did not know the religious context, and this is brought out by a deeper level of the structure. The first verse is a statement of the existential relationship of Kṛṣṇa to his devotees: he is necessary for life, as water to fish; he is desired and fulfilling, as moonbeams to *cakora* birds; he makes life meaningful and visible, as darkness does the stars. The second verse is an almost theological statement about the nature of Kṛṣṇa in his relation to his devotees, and to appreciate this a couple of things must be known. First, it is a very ancient image, that the relation between the metaphysical and the physical is the sky reflected in an earthen pot full of water. And secondly, that which is nonphysical has neither shadow nor image. Rādhā is then saying that Kṛṣṇa is true reality, and she herself is a mere reflection of this, without substance. She is also saying—and this is more important—that she and Kṛṣṇa are somehow one, as an entity and its reflection are one, essentially inseparable from one another. This has important implications. The third verse emphasizes this last point, saying that Rādhā, the devotee, is indelibly and permanently marked by the touch of Kṛṣṇa, with the implication that this is true in this life as in the ones to follow.

But the most important point is suggested by the last two lines, the signature lines or *bhanitā*, a custom of poets of the period. Throughout the poem Vidyāpati has been speaking as Rādhā. In the last two lines he speaks to Rādhā. But he still participates directly in his poem. This can be looked at in two ways. The first is that in much Indian thinking the word, the goddess Vāc, who participates directly in the creation, has truth as her nature. The poet then merely opens his mouth, so to speak, and truth emerges. But in the Vaiṣṇava context the situation is more complex. For the poet, when he speaks as Rādhā, or to Rādhā, has taken on a *bhāva,* he has taken on the nature of Rādhā or one of the Gopīs in the Bhāgavata story, in love with Kṛṣṇa. He does this in a variety of ways, which we shall examine shortly. The point at the moment is twofold. First, the expression of the condition of love or faith—usually the longing of separation—is through poetry. And secondly, it is on the immediate experience, expressed in this way, that doctrine is constructed. Let us look at another poem.

> The marks of fingernails are on your breast
> and my heart burns.
> Kohl of someone's eyes upon your lips
> darkens my face.
> I am awake all night;
> your eyes are red.
> So why do you entreat me, Kān,
> saying that you and I have but one heart?
> You come with choking voice
> while I want to weep.
> "Only our bodies are apart."
> But mine is light,
> and yours is dark.
> Go home, then,
> says Govindadāsa.[4]

The poem is extraordinarily tight and complex. There are one or two superficial things that ought to be noted. Fingernail marks on the breast are highly erotic both in meaning and in stimulus, according to the *Kāma-śāstra.* Kohl is that dark collyrium used by women as a cosmetic around the eyes and by women and children as medicinal ointment. Kān, or Kānu, is a pet name for Kṛṣṇa. And while Rādhā's body is golden in color, Kṛṣṇa's is *śyāma,* a dark emerald or deep blue-green color; this yields such highly erotic images as "the emerald set in the ring of gold."

But let us look again at the religious structure of the poem, leaving aside the formal characteristics. The poem comes from that section of the cycle called *māna*, meaning Rādhā's irritation and annoyance when she finds that Kṛṣṇa has been making love to other women; the expression of irritation, however, has a point. It is not mere subjective reaction, but is intended to coerce Kṛṣṇa back into his proper role of paying attention to her. This attitude, as we shall see, is both proper and improper. It is natural, for in any love relationship one is jealous of one's own position. At the same time, selfishness is a lesser order of passion than desiring the satisfaction of the object of love.

The *bhāva* of the poet is that of Rādhā, although the signature line is slightly ambiguous: when the poet says "Go home, then," he may be speaking as Rādhā to Kṛṣṇa. The other possibility is that he is speaking as the poet to both Rādhā and Kṛṣṇa. But whichever the case, the poem itself is clever and clear, and again to be read on several levels. The first one is the attribution of the characteristics of another to one's self. This is of course what *bhāva* means: that the worshiper takes on the characteristics of one of the persons of the Bhāgavata story. The second, however, is somewhat more subtle. It is like the form and the mirror-image in the other poem: Rādhā and Kṛṣṇa are in some indefinable way one, and what happens to one happens to the other. Yet if there is to be a love relationship, the two cannot be really one. "Only our bodies are apart": for a dynamic coming together, a restitution of the relationship of true love and its symbolically ecstatic result, there must be parts. But the poet says also that these parts are at the same time a whole.

The third and last poem points up some of these same matters, and adds a new dimension. It is structurally a very simple poem, and one of my favorites.

> Let the earth of my body be mixed with the earth
> my beloved walks on.
> Let the fire of my body be the brightness
> in the mirror that reflects his face.
> Let the water of my body join the waters
> of the lotus pool he bathes in.
> Let the breath of my body be air
> lapping his tired limbs.
> Let me be sky, and moving through me

that cloud-dark Śyāma, my beloved.

Govindadāsa says, O golden one,
Could he of the emerald body let you go.[5]

The images are striking, if rather conventional. The elements spoken of are the five elements of material nature, and on this level, borne out by the signature line, it seems that Rādhā either longs for dissolution or feels herself in the state, which, the textbooks of this sort of thing point out, is the penultimate state in a case of true love (the ultimate state). Another level is the purely erotic and highly sexual imagery of the last two lines of the poem itself, which is inescapable. The signature line is also erotic, speaking, as I mentioned before, of the metaphor of an emerald in a setting of gold. But the poem says other, deeper things. First of all, despite the extreme intimacy of such images as waters washing the body or the body and its breath, these relationships are not union. Other poets are fond of using such images as "fire and its flames" to describe the relationship, and here Govindadāsa too is saying that one element is of no use, or is meaningless, without the other. Secondly, the poet is saying that Rādhā is the material creature, and Kṛṣṇa the immaterial, needs the material to contain it and make it real and, if I might be permitted, potent. And the implications of this in turn are two: a) that Kṛṣṇa needs Rādhā, that God needs man; and that b) Kṛṣṇa can be known through the material being, that there is a direct link between the physical world, including the body, to the deity, and that therefore the material world, including the body, is real. This does two things. It makes erotic symbols more meaningful. It arouses the perhaps undefined feelings that if somehow one is related to the deity through the body itself, sexual imagery may be more than imagery. And it poses the problem that had to be faced by the theologians, who had the task of translating these ecstatic statements of faith into a system, of precisely how these relationships could be explained.

There is a saying in Bengal, possibly a mot of the late scholar Haraprasad Shastri, that *kānu bine gān nāi*, "without Kṛṣṇa there is no song." The story of the love of Rādhā and Kṛṣṇa has been so close to the surface of the consciousness of many Bengalis, be they Vaiṣṇava or Śākta, Hindu or Muslim, that many a love affair in literature finds itself under the shadow of this prototype. Except for the obviously Muslim name of the poet, the following lyric could easily have been written by one of the early, purely Vaiṣṇava devotees:

I die, burning in *viraha*;
where has he gone—Hari, dear to my heart?
I do not see his bending body on the banks of the
Kalindi,
or beneath the *kadamba* tree;
no more, in Vṛndāvana, does his flute call
his beloved Rādhā.

I lie in sleep, and see him in my dreams.
Awaking, I can only weep.
Vṛndāvana is empty; he who holds the flute
comes there no more.

Kāmar Āli, wretched, says:
the image of your beloved is in your mind.
Hari, dear to your heart,
will come and fill your eyes.[6]

But apart from devotional songs written by non-Vaiṣṇavas, the Rādhā-Kṛṣṇa theme has often been used as a point of departure for poetic reflections on a purely earthly love affair. Orthodox Vaiṣṇavas, of course, have their objections to such a use of the sacred theme. They have little sympathy from any point of view with such as the so-called kabiwallas, who flourished from the mid-eighteenth century to the end of the nineteenth. The usual view is that of S. K. De:

> This spiritual inadequacy of the songs of the Kabiwallas necessarily involved a lowering of the literary ideal.[7]

The kabiwallas were poets who extemporized upon a theme for the amusement, and sometimes the titillation, of their audience. For wealthy people in Calcutta, and in the houses of zamindari families outside the city, it was fashionable to hire two, or sometimes two groups, of these poets to entertain guests on festive occasions. The most colorful aspect of this custom was the *kabi-laṛāi* or verse-battle, a kind of flighting that has had a long and respectable history in India from the time of the poets in the court of King Vikramāditya; the two kabiwallas or sets of kabiwallas would exchange verses on a theme, a reward being given on the audience's judgment as to the better verses of the two. For a long time, it was the custom for the poets to decide the theme among themselves, before the contest began. And frequently the theme was an exchange between Rādhā and Kṛṣṇa, or between one of the other Gopīs and Rādhā. And since this theme was a familiar one, both audience and poets knew roughly what to expect. Later on, however, the exchanges grew more freewheeling, and yielded such as this, between Ṭhākur Sinha and, somewhat surprisingly, a Portuguese named Antony:

Ṭhākur Sinha:	Antony, I want to know this single thing: why do you wear such dress? Why don't you any longer wear a shirt?
Antony:	I am quite happy in Bengal, wearing a Bengali's dress; when your sister came into my bed I put aside my hat and shirt.

With increasing value being placed on surprise and shock, treatment of the Rādhā-Kṛṣṇa theme often became a little gross, and sometimes scurrilous.

In the late eighteenth century, the stream of Vaiṣṇava creativity had become a mere trickle. But although the primary motives, psychological and metaphysical, of the Vaiṣṇava tradition had all but disappeared from the scene, the poetic forms and conceits remained. The kabiwallas took the theme and to some extent the conventions of Vaiṣṇava religious poetry and made of it a poetry of secular love. Some of the results were appalling. They were no more than shallow mimicry of poets who, while not always themselves literarily brilliant, had at least the saving grace of substantial religious fervor. The lyric, secular, love poetry in the Sanskrit erotic anthologies, becoming religious with Bhartṛhari, reaching a zenith of devotional fervor in the songs of the Bengal

Vaiṣṇavas, had come full circle.

Although in the hands of some kabiwallas the Rādhā-Kṛṣṇa theme was a mockery, in the hands of others it took on a strange and interesting new life. When the old Vaiṣṇavas spoke of Rādhā, they meant both Rādhā the woman participating in a love affair, and Rādhā the symbol of the human soul. The kabiwallas did not concern themselves overly with symbolism. Intheir eyes, Rādhā's love was not a state of grace; like that of any young person, Rādhā's love brought with it pain and lust and general confusion.

> When I was a girl, I was happy.
> I did not desire happiness.
> I knew no lover, nor did I know the joys of love;
> the lotus of my heart was closed.
> But now the hundred-petalled lotus, closed and warm,
> has been opened
> by the touch of time.[8]

Or again, very much in the spirit of Hāla's Prakrit verse:

> My heart aches, my friend,
> that what I had to say to him remains unsaid,
> for modesty.[9]

"Spiritually inadequate" though these songs may be, they have a warmth and directness too often lacking in those closer to the classical conventions:

> He is mine! I am young, and spring has come,
> and he is in another land.
> But when, at last, he comes laughing to me,
> and when I see him laugh, and swim in my tears,
> how can I refuse him?
> My heart longs to hold him to my breast,
> though my modesty says no.[10]

As devotional religion gained predominance in the medieval times, the religious and erotic blended imperceptibly with one another. Circumambulating this poetry of love, the Vaiṣṇavas saw it one way, the kabiwallas another. The duality is inherent; in Rabindranath Tagore's English *Gitanjali*, the book that moved Yeats and Pound to such extravagant praise, it seems to be Rādhā who speaks, just as she spoke in the sixteenth century:

> Clouds heap upon clouds, and it darkens. Ah, love, why dost thou let me wait outside at the door all alone?
> In the busy moments of the noontide work I am with the crowd, but on this dark lonely day it is only for thee that I hope.
> If thou showest me not thy face, if thou leavest me wholly aside, I know not how I am to pass these long rainy hours.
> I keep on gazing at the far gleam of the sky, and my heart wanders wailing with the restless wind.[11]

NOTES

1. John Frederick Mims, *The Poems of St. John of the Cross* (New York: Grove Press, 1959), p. 21.
2. Quoted in Moshe Lazar, *Amour courtois et "fin 'amors" dans la litterature du XII siècle* (Paris: Librairie C. Klincksieck, 1964), p. 72.
3. Edward C. Dimock, Jr., and Denise Levertov, *In Praise of Krishna* (New York: Doubleday, 1967), p. 17.
4. Ibid., p. 45.
5. Ibid., p. 58.
6. Yatīndramohan Bhattācāryya, *Bāṅgālār vaiṣṇava bhāvāpanna musulman kavi* (Calcutta: Book Society of India, 1950).
7. Sushil Kumar De, *Bengali Literature in the Nineteenth Century*, 2nd ed. (Calcutta: Firma K. L. Mukhopadhyaya, 1962), p. 295.
8. Bengali text quoted, ibid., p. 343.
9. Bengali text quoted, ibid.
10. Bengali text quoted, ibid., p. 342.
11. Rabindranath Tagore, *Gitanjali* (New York: Macmillan, 1913). Quoted in Amiya Chakravarti, *A Tagore Reader* (New York: Macmillan, 1961), p. 297.

Dēvī Shrines and Folk Hinduism in Medieval Tamilnad

Burton Stein

श्रीः Two decades ago, the noted South Indian archaeologist K. R. Srinivasan presented a paper on goddess shrines in early South Indian temples in which he pointed out that from the thirteenth century, these shrines, called *kāmākōṭṭam* or *tirukāmākōṭṭam,* were a prominent feature of Hindu temple worship in Tamil country.[1] Neither Srinivasan nor other scholars who have written on early South Indian religion have offered explanations for this development in the thirteenth century;[2] one is proposed here.

Essentially, the argument is that the prominence given to *dēvī,* or goddess worship, from the thirteenth century marked a significant universalization of folk ritual; it was part of a larger social process involving the insertion of folk elements into the highest levels of cultural activities. Among the most important of these activities, in addition to *dēvī* worship, were the full emergence of the temple as a popular pilgrimage center and the development of centers of learning and religious instruction under the direction of peasant caste (Śūdra) savants.

From the point of view of the development of a major variant of Hinduism—that of Tamilnad (Tamiḻnāḍu)—it is of some importance to account for transformations of older forms of ritual and the emergence of new ones. In much that is written on the history of Indian religion, there has been a tendency to regard developments of the sort examined here as a "natural" unfolding of the logic of doctrine in ritual. Thus, it is considered as unexceptional that the devotional (*bhakti*) forms of orthopraxy should come to include the intensified worship of female deities. It had to come sometime; why not the thirteenth century? This is certainly an unacceptable historical position. Hinduism in its various regional forms must be viewed as resulting from the activities of men concerned with their own salvation as their conception of a *dharmic* universe, with their livelihoods as well as their fulfillment as teachers and sacrificers; in short, their concern with the exigent as well as the transcendent. The very variety of religious forms enveloped by the label, "Hinduism," is perhaps the clearest proof that emergent doctrines and practices are founded in historical processes. There is, after all, persuasive evidence of decision and selection in the development of Hindu doctrines and practices, some of which being favored for a time—as the Pāśupata, Kāpālika, and Kālāmukha sects of Śaivites—but, in South India at least, failing to continue as popular forms despite impressive early careers.[3] Hence, attempting to explain the significant place that came to be occupied by the worship of goddesses after the thirteenth century in Tamil country means addressing the historical process from which such a form emerged. It is attempting to understand the larger cultural whole of which goddess worship was but part.

Toward such an understanding, the identification of the female deity with folk forms of religion bears consideration. The forms of ritual and doctrine about which most is known in South India and elsewhere in the subcontinent are the high purāṇic forms.[4] The great sects of the medieval period trace their origins from popularizing, devotional hymnists through learned men who sought to reconcile devotional religion (*bhakti*) with the legacy of philosophical and ritual principles enshrined in the major *purāṇas*. These older Sanskrit works dwell upon the personalities of the deities Viṣṇu and Śiva in their many manifestations; they preserve doctrinal and philosophical ideas from the Upaniṣads and are thus linked to the Vedic wellsprings of Hindu orthodoxy; and, after the eighth century, these works came under the special protective custody of Brahmans as sufficient sources of orthodoxy related to salvation through devotion. Sanskrit, Brahmans, and the great male gods (*mahādēvas*) are among the prime markers of the devotional religion of the *purāṇas*. Yet, the religious allegiance of most South Indians was via liturgy in vernacular languages and priests drawn from respectable groups of peasants, as well as those of lower status, to a deity whose nature—while conceived as personal and devotional—was in most cases female.[5] That this disjunction between the folk and purāṇic modes was not perfect may be admitted without negating the distinction.[6] Prior to the thirteenth century there were certainly those among the higher levels of the non-Brahman peasantry who learned Sanskrit and, with it, gained access to the higher forms of religion and thought associated with that language. Moreover, the services of Brahman ritual functionaries of the purāṇic tradition must have extended to respectable non-Brahmans from whom the basic material support to purāṇic Hindu institutions came. These limiting factors notwithstanding, the purāṇic forms as practiced in the relatively few Brahmanical temple centers of the pre-thirteenth century (e.g., Kāñcīpuram, Tiruvoṟṟiyūr, and Chidambaram [Citamparam] or Tiḷḷai), as well as in the more numerous Brahman settlements (*brahmadēyas*) in the Coromandel plain, were much removed from the enduring commitment of most peasants to nonpurāṇic religious activities involving female deities. It is the closing of this gap between purāṇic and folk forms of religion and the conditions surrounding that development during and after the thirteenth century that bears special examination.

Prior to the thirteenth century, separate shrines to a purāṇic goddess (*dēvī*), while not unknown as part of a temple complex, were rare. *Dēvī* images within a temple, but not separately sheltered, became common from at least the eighth century, according to extant epigraphical evidence and *āgama* texts of the time.[7] Among the most important of such deities were Durgā, a major Śiva deity, Jyēṣṭhā, the fearsome sister of the benign Lakṣmī of Viṣṇu association, and the "Seven Mothers" (Sapta-mātṛka). Durgā shrines can be identified at Mahābalipuram perhaps as early as the late seventh century, at Paṉamalai during the eighth century, and at Tirupparaṅkuṉṟam in Tanjore in about 850 A.D.[8] Jyēṣṭhā was separately enshrined in a cave near Madurai in the eighth century, and, according to early Chola (Cōḻa) inscriptions, at Tirukkaṭṭalai (Pudukkōṭṭai) and Tirupparāytturai (Tiruchirāpaḷḷi) as well as Eṟumbūr (Eṟumūr, South Arcot) in 1039 A.D.[9] There were separate shrines of the "Seven Mothers" at Ālambākkam (Tiruchirāpaḷḷi) of the early ninth century and at Vēḷachēri and Tiruttaṇi in modern Chingleput district of the early and middle tenth century.[10] Though purāṇic goddesses were thus occasionally enshrined separately in Pallava and early Chola temples, after the eleventh century the goddess Pārvatī or Umā supplanted them as the favored goddess.[11] Pārvatī became the most popular goddess worshipped in later times as Ammaṉ, "mother"; but she does not appear to have been accorded separate shrines in Pallava and Chola temples. The earliest reliable reference to Ammaṉ shrines dates from the eleventh century with inscriptions of Rājēndracōḻa I's time at Kandiyūr and Eṇṇāyiram.[12] Inscriptions of the late eleventh, twelfth, and thirteenth centuries refer specifically to other Ammaṉ shrines established throughout Tamil country.[13]

Thus, though not numerous when compared with the major male deities for whom shrines existed in Tamil country, those devoted to goddesses did exist. Ammaṉ shrines, those devoted to Pārvatī or Umā, gradually displaced other older *dēvī* shrines after the eleventh century, and, after the thirteenth century, most Śiva temples in Tamil country had such a shrine.[14] The thirteenth century and after—the twilight years of the great Cholas—witnessed a period of prodigious temple building sometimes classified by the architectural stylistic label of "Pāṇḍyan" or "Later Chola."[15] Much of this temple construction was spurred by the spread of a revitalized Viṣṇu worship as well as Śiva worship. In fact this period was one in which Vaiṣṇavite religious centers began a growth cycle that culminated in the Vijayanagar period of the sixteenth century. *Dēvī* worship was as significant among Vaiṣṇavites as Śaivites, and one of the elements that distinguished the two often competitive traditions—the Vaikhānasāgama and Pāñcarātrāgama—among Tamil Vaiṣṇavite ritual specialists was the place to be accorded female deities who were regarded as consorts (*nācciyār*) of the god Viṣṇu.[16] Such consorts of Viṣṇu included Lakṣmī as most important; others were: Āṇḍāḷ (also called "Sudikkoḍutta Nācciyār") at the much-visited shrine in in Śrīvilluputtūr in Ramnād;[17] the Chenchu Nācciyār at the Ahobilam Narasimhaswāmi shrine in modern Vizagapatnam district; the Malayalam Nācciyār shrine in Kāñcīpuram; and the Uraiyūr

Vaḷḷi Nācciyār shrine at the premier Viṣṇu temple of Tamilnad at Śrīraṅgam.[18] As in the case of the Śiva goddesses, the Viṣṇu consorts characteristically took their names from the male deity with whom they were related in the *nāyikā-nāyaka*—loved and lover—type of *bhakti* relationship: the principal deity at the great Tanjore temple, Bṛhadīśvara (Peruvuḍaiyar) had his Bṛhannāyakī (Peruyanāyaki), Raṅganātha (at Śrīraṅgam) had Raṅganāyakī, Sundareśvara (at Madurai) had Mīnākṣī, Ēkāmrēśvara (at Kāñchīpuram) had Kāmākṣī.[19] In some cases at least, these shrines have been more popularly known for the consort than for the principal lord to whom they were attached, namely, Mīnākṣī, Bṛhannāyakī, and Kāmākṣī, and it is probable that the generic term, *kāmākōṭṭam*, was derived from the most famous of the *dēvīs*, Kāmākṣī in Kāñcīpuram.[20]

In whatever other ways the principle of female deity in South Indian Hinduism is considered, the association with folk religion must be regarded as important. Scholarly opinion is that worship of the goddess probably has deep roots in prehistoric Indian religion, predating the introduction of Aryan forms of worship and never fully displaced in the theological consciousness of the high tradition. In the context of Aryan religion this ancient mother-goddess element is preserved in the principle of *śakti*, the active and generative element of the godhead, where it provides a potentially significant ritual place for the female deity. In the *Mahābhārata* epic, Durgā, the prototypic goddess, is seen as the spouse of Śiva (as Umā) and identified with the Vedas and Upaniṣads as a pure god-force.[21] However, in other contexts, the female principle is seen as somewhat sinister and foreboding. Durgā is thus also depicted in *Mahābhārata* as a virgin deity delighting in wine, flesh, and animal sacrifice.[22] Similarly, hovering on the edges of certain forms of early Śiva worship that have tended to be eclipsed by later forms of Śaivite *bhakti* (again, the Pāśupatas and Kāpālikas) the darker side of this active female principle appears to have been preserved.[23]

However, the female deity has been most perfectly preserved in folk religion; village deities worshipped in South India have been goddesses—*grāma dēvatās* to whom animals and in former times humans were sacrificed.[24] To these sturdy objects of peasant worship, male attendants are at times admitted to a rough parity, as in the case of Ayyanar (Iyenar), but usually the latter are considered as guardians of the female shrines and subordinate to the *grāma dēvatā*.[25] In some of the cases referred to above, as in the Chenchu-, Malayalam-, and Uraiyūr Vaḷḷi Nācciyār, it appears quite clear that early folk deities, patronesses of ancient folk religions, later enjoyed a universalization of status in being made consorts of purāṇic deities.[26]

It is, moreover, probable that folk goddesses had come to enjoy considerable prestige and support beyond the confines of villages in early Chola times only to be neglected—perhaps even deliberately displaced—during the period of the great Cholas. The research of Dr. Suresh Pillai on the Kāvērī basin during the reigns of Rājarājacōḻa and Rājēndracōḻa (ca. 985–1050 A.D.) strongly argues such a view.[27] In his special study of the Rājarājēśvaram (or Bṛhadīśvara) temple in modern Tanjore, he shows that endowments of Rājarāja I's time were wholly in support of "canonical" (or "purāṇic," as I have used it here) male deities, most of whom were manifestations of Śiva;[28] he also argues that the exclusive favor shown to purāṇic deities has obscured the extent to which folk goddesses had occupied significant local dominance before the completion of the temple at Tanjore. From the inscriptional record of canonical endowments, Suresh Pillai is able to provide references to shrines to *piḍāris*, *kāḍukāls*, and *naṅgais*, then and now female folk deities in the vicinity of Tanjore. An indication of the wealth and importance of these shrines is that Rājarāja demanded that hundreds of temple dancing girls and musicians of these shrines serve the god Bṛhadīśvara in the temple that he built.[29] From this and other evidence, he concludes that Rājarāja followed a policy of "Aryanization" or "canonization"[30] of those religious activities with which he and his family associated themselves, and for a time, the worship of noncanonical deities was subject to "deliberate suppression."[31] However, he also points to the rise of Umā shrines and later, at the time of Kulōttuṅga III, the establishment of *nācciyār* shrines that suggest necessary royal concessions to the continued popularity of folk-goddess worship.

The proliferation of temples during the later Chola age—the thirteenth century and after—is itself a development indicating a greater degree of popular participation in *bhakti* ritual. As temples rose in Tamil country, the principal former site of high ritual, the Brahman village, or *brahmadēya*, declined. There is ample evidence that fewer villages were granted to groups of Brahman families for support of teaching and ritual activities.[32] During the early and middle periods of Chola rule, that is, the ninth to the twelfth century, *brahmadēyas* were the prime centers of Vedic ritual. Here there were numerous small shrines, to Śiva primarily, but also to Viṣṇu, where learned Brahmans and their ritual practices prevailed. Uttaramērūr, in modern Chingleput district, had seven Vedic shrines during its period of greatest importance; five were Śiva shrines, and two were devoted to Viṣṇu. According to an inscription of 1037 A.D., Eṇṇāyiram in modern South Arcot had twelve Vedic and village shrines.[33] It is probable that the modes of worship at most such shrines eschewed the more popular forms of *bhakti*. K. R. Srinivasan has indeed suggested that in about 800 A.D., there was a reversal of earlier Śaivite forms of iconic worship, and the replacement of anthropomorphic images with the aniconic Śiva *liṅga*.[34] The new temple then, with its female as well as male deities, its relatively greater accessibility for ordinary folk than the precincts of the Brahman quarters of villages, its more overt appeal to the emotional sensibilities of devotees than to their minds, and its explicit effort to create a mood of the most intense religiosity, came increasingly to be the major locus of *bhakti* religion after the thirteenth century.

Temples were established at existing folk-pilgrimage places, or, occasionally, Brahman villages were transformed in their character, and often their names, by the expansion of one of their shrines to the status of a major *bhakti* pilgrimage center. In either of these events, the decline of the *brahmadēya* was inevitable. The pioneer work of R. Sathianathaier[35] and more recent research by the author make it certain that these unique, prestigeful, rural settlements of Brahmans ceased to be established after the twelfth century except for a few in the marginal southern territories of the resurgent Pāṇḍyas. Not only were the multiform sacral functions of such settlements assumed by temples, but, as significantly, the intellectual and training activities through which the high Brahmanical traditions had been maintained in Tamil country were now challenged by a vigorous, non-Brahman, intellectual, and reflective reform movement, Śaiva Siddhānta,[36] to which further reference is made below.

Contemporary with and perhaps underlying the changes in religion and learning outlined above, there occurred a fundamental change in the society and politics of Tamilnad during the twelfth and thirteenth centuries. Territorially segmented polities and societies of Tamil country that had been loosely integrated by the Chola overlordship of the tenth to twelfth centuries attained a degree of strength that not only made the Chola state unstable and ultimately contributed to its end, but also provided the basis for the full assertion of the cultural and religious preferences of peasant leadership of the numerous localities of Tamil country at the time. One important consequence of this social change was the rise to a prominence not previously enjoyed of the female folk deities of the peasantry.

Social transformations that produced, among other things, changes in the religious institutions of Tamil country during the thirteenth century can only be outlined here.[37]

Between the tenth and thirteenth centuries, Tamil culture and society was fragmented into hundreds of local territorial segments called "*nāḍus*." Within each of these localities a dominant peasant group called "*nāṭṭār*," "those of the *nāḍu*," exercised secular dominance through their control over cultivable land, the agrarian relations revolving about such land, and their hold over chieftainships representing local authority. In each such territorial segment, there were settlements of Brahmans in *brahmadēyas* enjoying high local prestige and considerable autonomy; within each locality there were also settlements specializing in trade and artisan production, though localized trade and handicraft production was ubiquitous in the large, pluralistic peasant settlements of the time.

Tying these hundreds of localities together were some overarching elements. First, there was a political structure, the Chola state. Conventionally discussed as a unitary and bureaucratic political system, the Chola state was actually a "segmentary state"[38] in which secular authority was widely distributed over hundreds of *nāṭṭār* groups, each of which enjoyed private territorial jurisdiction while recognizing the overlordship of the Chola ruler. The latter was essentially *primus inter pares*—the most powerful *nāṭṭār* of the Tamil region; his superiority was based on the fact that his locality was the large, populous, and fertile lower Kāvērī basin, the greatest power base in South India. Cōḻanāḍu warriors had one other exceptional attribute that distinguished them from the class of locally dominant peasant folk over whom their overlordship extended: they made astute use of an ancient tribal kingship as a source of legitimacy for integrating the loose segmentary system of power to which their name was lent. This legitimacy and its political and ideological uses was largely symbolic, involving the use of Brahmans and their special status and skills in the manipulation of symbols. The best products of this use and skill are the thousands of copper and stone inscriptions spread over a substantial portion of South India from the tenth to the thirteenth centuries.

A second overarching element in the structure of Tamil society and culture of the pre-thirteenth century were the Brahmans. Most Brahmans lived in large peasant villages along with artisans and traders. These Brahmans would thus have been fully integrated members of localized, rural societies though possessing relatively high prestige attached to their sacral functions as to their educational activities.[39] The value of these contributions to local society may be appreciated from the quality of support extended by the dominant peasant communities within whose territories they lived. In almost every locality (*nāḍu*) of Tamil country, which during the tenth to thirteenth centuries extended into what is now southern Kerala (then, Vēnāḍu) and Mysore (then, Gaṅgāvādi), there was at least one large settlement in which numerous Brahman families were domiciled and under whose assembly (*mahāsabhā*) the village and its environs were managed.[40] These great Brahman settlements were the most important centers of ritual and learning; it was here that the high tradition of Hinduism and Sanskrit learning was preserved in Tamilnad as well as for a good part of the rest of South India. The resources for and the protection of Brahmans, whether those scattered throughout peasant villages of the Tamil region or concentrated in the several hundred *brahmadēyas* of the region, came from the dominant peasantry who controlled the *nāḍus*. That this support and protection was voluntary is indisputable; it was a direct reflection of the mutual interests of both groups—Brahmans and peasants.[41]

The result of this relationship was to disseminate over most of the Tamil region a homogeneous high culture involving the worship of Vedic gods and the support of Sanskrit learning. Even beyond this, however, there was a secondary homogenization of Tamil culture that resulted in part from the degree of integration of Brahmans in Tamil society, but also because much of the high Sanskrit learning that influenced Tamil culture was brought within the competence of non-Brahmans so as to create a more elegant, and highly Sanskritized, Tamil culture borne by respectable non-Brahmans as well as Brahmans.

It is with respect to these two broadly integrating elements in Tamil country—the segmentary Chola state and the increasingly elegant Tamil culture, deeply informed by Sanskrit learning—that explanations of the transformations first evident in the thirteenth century are based.

The once great Chola overlordship had extended from Cape Comorin to the Tungabhadrā River, but, during the twelfth century, the Chola capacity to exercise such a sweeping overlordship was undermined from within and without. The latter has certainly been noticed by historians, for contemporary inscriptions bear witness to the serious inroads upon and, finally, the extinction of the Chola tributary overlordship by Pāṇḍyan and Hoysala warriors. This reversal of predatory patterns of warfare—essentially pillaging expeditions—upon the Chola heartland of the Kāvērī basin heralded the maturity of two regions abutting upon the Tamil plain that long had suffered the incursions of Chola warriors and a degree of new settlement from Chola country. Now it was the former victims together with a resurgent Ceylon, which had also felt the weight of Chola raids, who turned on the Cholas.

Less well recognized in the collapse of the Chola state were changes in the political system of Tamil country. During the twelfth century, segmentary units of power that exceeded any of the previous centuries of the Chola overlordship had come into existence. These were supralocalities —several localities (*nāḍus*) cooperating closely under an assembly of *nāṭṭārs* called the "*periyanāḍu*." Such supralocal bodies assumed responsibility for temples, Brahman settlements, and exercised control over itinerant trade guilds that moved over much of the southern peninsula.[42] It is noteworthy that the standard verses introducing the inscriptional words of the supralocal assembly (*periyanāḍu*) offer worship to and seek the special protection of the earth goddess (Bhūmi-dēvī) whose shrines were of special importance.[43] Like the older *nāṭṭār*—dominant peasant groups of the numerous localities into which Tamil country was divided—the *nāṭṭār* of the thirteenth century were the leaders of local society. They were ceremonial chieftains with respect to the dominant peasant groups to which they belonged and, on behalf of such hereditary hierarchies of peasant folk, they managed the small territorial polities comprising diverse, ranked groups from Brahmans to the lowest: recent migrants from the forests who occupied the basest status. Unlike the older *nāṭṭār*, however, those of the thirteenth century had found the organizational means to achieve enlarged cooperating subregions of localities. Related to this new ability and confidence were religious and intellectual aspects of Tamil culture as it had come to develop by the thirteenth century.

One important sign of the quality of this culture was the Śaiva Siddhānta movement; another was the establishment of non-Brahman seminaries (*maṭhas*) for propagation of the Śaiva message. It is unnecessary to discuss the Śaiva Siddhānta movement, for it is well described in the learned literature. What must be emphasized here is that the major early figures in the philosophical and religious development were of non-Brahman, peasant origin. Meykaṇḍar and Maṟai, the first and third leaders of this movement were *veḷḷāḷa*;[44] Umāpati, the last of the great early teachers of the Siddhānta, of the late thirteenth century, was a Brahman of Chidambaram who was allegedly excommunicated from his natal caste for association with the *veḷḷāḷa gurus* of the movement.[45] Also to be noted is the tradition that Meykaṇḍar translated from Sanskrit to Tamil twelve major works under the title of the *Śiva-jñāna-bōdham*. This, with other evidence of the period, indicates that some of peasant status were educated to high competence in Sanskrit.[46]

Seminaries modelled upon Brahman *maṭhas* became centers for the Śaiva Siddhānta movement, and these centers were under the guidance of non-Brahman *gurus* carrying forward the work of the *veḷḷāḷa* founders. An elaborate system of *maṭha* organization emerged in the early thirteenth century, the headquarters of a line of teachers being in one place—usually in Tanjore where the Sanskritization of non-Brahman savants appears to have gone furthest—with branches at considerable distances. For example, the Māḷigai-maṭha at Tiruvidaimarudūr, in modern Tanjore district, had one of its branches at Chidambaram (Tiḷḷai) in modern South Arcot.[47] Such *maṭhas*, or *guhais* as learned centers for non-Brahman ascetics were called, may not have replicated in full the learned traditions of contemporary Brahman *maṭhas* about which many things are known, but they are impressive signs of the degree of confidence in their learning possessed by members of the dominant peasant groups of Tamil country at the time.

It is against this background of social and cultural change involving segments of the Tamil peasantry during the twelfth and thirteenth centuries that the expansion of *dēvī* shrines must be understood and the timing appreciated. That the explanation offered here is somewhat labored is recognized. However, because changes in Hindu ritual are usually not attended by contemporary explanations and justifications (unlike, for example, crises in western Christianity at about the same time), it is often only by indirection and inference that the significance of such changes can be perceived. Other scholars have noted the relationship between the development of *dēvī* shrines into prominent architectural and ritual components of medieval Tamil Hinduism and folk forms of religion: notably the perceptive Dr. V. Rāghavan,[48] T. K. Viraraghavachari,[49] Dr. Suresh Pillai[50] as mentioned above, and the epigraphist and iconographic scholar, P. R. Srinivasan.[51] More can and should be done to trace these changes. Iconographic and inscriptional evidence relating to them is available.

The attempt here to place such a significant development in the appropriate complex, historical setting of its emergence must be regarded as preliminary until more detailed surveys are undertaken. The forms of *bhakti* Hinduism of India's medieval past are rich and varied; they offer much to scholars who seek understanding of the society and culture of the time. But, these forms do not spring forth solely from an interior logic; they also result from the decisions and actions of pious and not-so-pious men searching for the means of symbolizing and attaining the grace that *bhakti* promises, and reflect their needs as men living in real society and time.

NOTES

1. K. R. Srinivasan, "Tirukāmakōṭṭām," *Proceedings of the All-India Oriental Conference, Nagpur, 1946* (Lucknow: Sarfaray Quami Press, 1946). Also see his later paper dealing with this and related matters: *Some Aspects of Religion as Revealed by Early Monuments and Literature in the South*. Sankara Parvati Endowment Lectures, 1959–60 (Madras: University of Madras, 1960).

2. Viz.: R. G. Bhandarkar, *Vaiṣṇavism, Śaivism, and Minor Religious Systems* (Poona: Bhandarkar Oriental Research Institute, 1928); K. A. Nilakanta Sastri, *Development of Religion in South India* (Madras: Orient Longmans, 1963); T. A. Gopinatha Rao, *Elements of Hindu Iconography*, vol. 1, pt. 2, chapter entitled "Devi" (New York: Paragon Book Reprint Corp., 1969); M. Rajamanickam, *The Development of Śaivism in South India (A.D. 300–1300)* (Dharmapuram: Dharmapuram Adhinam, 1964); and B. Suresh [Pillai], "Historical and Cultural Geography and Ethnography of South India" (Ph.D. thesis, Deccan College Post-Graduate and Research Institute, Poona, 1965) and his "Raajaraajeesvaram at Tancaavuur," *Proceedings of the First International Conference of Tamil Studies, Kuala Lumpur, 1966* (Kuala Lumpur: International Association of Tamil Research, 1968), pp. 437–50.

3. Sastri, *Development of Religion in South India*, pp. 62–63.

4. Ibid., where Sastri says almost nothing of folk religion.

5. Generally recognized, e.g., ibid., p. 65; more comprehensively explored in Henry Whitehead, *The Village Gods of South India* (Calcutta, London, New York: Oxford University Press, 1921).

6. E.g., the *pañcāyatana* worship of Śaivites in South India include: Śiva, Viṣṇu, Gaṇeśa, Sūrya, *and Dēvī*, J. N. Farquhar, *An Outline of the Religious Literature of India* (London: H. Milford, Oxford University Press, 1920), p. 293.

7. Srinivasan, *Some Aspects of Religion*, p. 22.

8. Ibid., pp. 28–29; Rao, *Elements of Hindu Iconography*, vol. 1, pt. 2, pp. 391–92.

9. Srinivasan, *Some Aspects of Religion*, pp. 26–27.

10. Ibid., pp. 24–26.

11. Srinivasan, "Tirukāmakōṭṭām," p. 52.

12. Ibid., pp. 53–56; Rajamanickam, *Development of Śaivism*, pp. 180–81.

13. Enumerated in Srinivasan, "Tirukāmakōṭṭām," p. 56. Also see Rajamanickam, *Development of Śaivism*, pp. 180–81.

14. Srinivasan, "Tirukāmakōṭṭām," p. 56.

15. Government of India, *Census of India, 1961*, vol. 9, "Madras," pt. 11-D, "Temples of Madras State; Chingleput District and Madras City," comp. P. K. Nambiar and N. Krishnamurthy (1965), p. 7. Also, S. R. Balasu-

brahmanyam, *Early Chola Art*, pt. 1 (Bombay: Asia Publishing House, 1966), especially p. 253 ff. for his discussion of periods of early temple styles; James C. Harle, *Temple Gateways in South India; the Architecture and Iconography of the Cidambaram Gopuras* (Oxford: Bruno Cassirer, 1963), pp. xii–xiii.

16. Sastri, *Development of Religion*, p. 67.

17. T. K. Vīrāghavāchāri, "The Srivilliputtur Temple of Sudikoḍutta Nacciyar," *Tirumalai-Tirupati Devasthanam Bulletin*, no. 6.

18. Ibid., 6, no. 5:5–6; V. Rāghavan, "Variety and Integration in the Pattern of Indian Culture," *Far Eastern Quarterly* 15, no. 4 (1956):500.

19. Srinivasan, *Some Aspects of Religion*, pp. 32–33.

20. Ibid. Also see Bhandarkar's discussion of the term *kāmakalā* as a form of deity according to the *śākta* doctrine of *śambhava-darśana*, in which Śiva and Śakti are combined (*Vaiṣṇavism, Śaivism*, pp. 207–8).

21. Bhandarkar, *Vaiṣṇavism, Śaivism*, pp. 203 ff.; Farquhar, *Religious Literature of India*, pp. 149–50.

22. Bhandarkar, *Vaiṣṇavism, Śaivism*, pp. 203 ff.; Farquhar, *Religious Literature of India*, pp. 149–50; Sastri, *Development of Religion*, p. 65.

23. Sastri, *Development of Religion*, p. 63; Bhandarkar, *Vaiṣṇavism, Śaivism*, pp. 181–83 and 206.

24. Whitehead, *Village Gods of South India*, pp. 17–18 and 82; Sastri, *Development of Religion*, p. 65.

25. Whitehead, *Village Gods of South India*, p. 18, and passim. This is interestingly reflected in the early iconography of the "Seven Mothers" where Gaṇeśa and Śiva as Vīrabhadra flank the female figures as their protectors (Rao, *Hindu Iconography*, 2, pt. 2:377 ff.).

26. Vīrāghavāchāri, "The Srivilliputtur Temple of Sudikkoḍutta Nacciyar"; Raghavan, "Variety and Integration in the Pattern of Indian Culture"; Suresh Pillai, "Raajaraajeesvaram at Tancaavuur," p. 443.

27. Suresh Pillai, "Raajaraajeesvaram at Tancaavuur," p. 443.

28. Ibid., pp. 438–39, noting the following Śiva images: Kalyaṇasundarar, Dakshiṇāmūrti, Liṅgapurāṇadevar, Āṭavallār (Naṭarājā), and Ardhanārī; mentioned as less significant were: Sūrya, Brahma, Viṣṇu, and Subrahmaṇya.

29. Ibid., pp. 441–43.

30. Suresh Pillai used the term "aryanization" frequently in his thesis, "Historical and Cultural Geography," pp. ii, 134, 287, 291, and especially, pp. 323 ff. In the article, however, the term "canonization" is used.

31. Ibid., p. 450.

32. R. Sathianathaier, "Studies in the Ancient History of Tondamandalam," The Sankara-Parvati Endowment Lectures, 1943–44 (Madras: University of Madras, 1944). More recent work by the present writer corroborates and extends Sathianathaier's findings; it forms a part of a larger work on the peasant agrarian order of medieval South India.

33. K. A. Nilakanta Sastri, *Studies in Cola History and Administration* (Madras: University of Madras, 1932), pp. 85 and 101; Dr. B. S. Baliga, ed., *Madras District Gazetteers: South Arcot* (Madras: Government of Madras, 1962), p. 483.

34. Srinivasan, "Some Aspects of Religion," p. 62.

35. Note 32, above.

36. This movement in Tamilnad had much in common with the Vīra Śaiva movement in Karṇāṭaka at the same time; see Bhandarkar's discussion of the two (*Vaiṣṇavism, Śaivism*, pp. 187–200).

37. A general statement on these transformations may be found in the present writer's exploratory essay: "Integration of the Agrarian System of South India," in *Land Control and Social Structure in Indian History*, ed. Robert E. Frykenberg (Madison: University of Wisconsin Press, 1969), pp. 175 ff. Note should be taken of the differences that the author has come to make between the early and later period of the Cholas.

38. The concept of the "segmentary state" has been most fully utilized by A. W. Southall; see his *Alur Society* (Cambridge: At the University Press, 1953), pp. 238–52.

39. The quality of Brahman society and culture in Tamil country is well covered in the various works of Nilakanta Sastri. A recent and interesting new view of this matter, in which Brahmans are seen as closely integrated with the general society, is that of Dr. N. Subrahmaniam in a series of lectures delivered at the University of Madras in 1967 entitled "Brahmans in South India." These lectures should be published by the University of Madras within the near future.

40. Published historical accounts of this institution tend to focus on the most famous of the Chola *brahmadēyas*, Uttaramērūr, which is regarded as typical of the class and is highly questionable. See K. A. Nilakanta Sastri's discussion in his *Studies in Cola History* and that of K. V. Subrahmanva Aiver's in his *Historical Sketches of the Ancient Dekhan* (Coimbatore: K. S. Vaidyanathan, 1967), 2:209 ff.

41. Burton Stein, "Brahman and Peasant in Early South Indian History," *Adyar Library Bulletin*, 31–32 (1967–68; Dr. V. Rāghavan Felicitation Volume):229–69.

42. Burton Stein, "Medieval Coromandel Trade," in *Merchants and Scholars; Essays in the History of Exploration and Trade*, ed. John Parker (Minneapolis: University of Minnesota Press, 1965), pp. 47–62.

43. The most complete published analysis of the *periyanāḍu* and its inscriptions is: K. V. Subrahmanya Aiyer, "The Largest Provincial Organizations in India," *Quarterly Journal of the Mythic Society*, n.s. 15, no. 1:29–47; no. 2:70–98; no. 4:270–86; 46, no. 1:8–22. Note should be taken of the discussion of Bhūmidēvī or Bhūdēvī, the earth goddess and consort of Viṣṇu in Rao, *Elements of Hindu Iconography*, 2, pt. 2:375.

44. K. R. Srinivasa Iyengar, "Dravidian Language and Literature; Śaiva Siddhānta Literature," in *History and Culture of the Indian People*, ed. R. C. Majumdar (Bombay: Bharatiya Vidya Bhavan, 1966), 5:366.

45. Farquhar, *Religious Literature of India*, p. 257; Sastri, *Development of Religion*, p. 94.

46. Violet Paranjoti, *Śaiva Siddhānta in the Meykaṇḍar Śāstra* (London: Luzac, 1938) contains a list of important sect works.

47. Rajamanickam, *The Development of Śaivism*, p. 232. Cf. also, Government of India, *Annual Report for South Indian Epigraphy, 1909* (Madras, 1910), par. 53, pp. 103–5.

48. Rajamanickam, *The Development of Śaivism*, p. 232.

49. Ibid.

50. Suresh Pillai, "Raajaraajeesvaram at Tancaavuur," p. 450.

51. Personal communication during the writer's stay in Mysore at the Office of the Government Epigraphist, Government of India.

Prolegomenon to a Cultural History of the Gangetic Civilization

Barrie M. Morrison

श्रीः For the past three years I have been collecting data for a study of the evolution of the Gangetic civilization. During this time I have been hard pressed to find or devise an analytical and descriptive model to order the immense array of information into some comprehensible and aesthetic whole. There are models available that appear to offer plausible categories for ordering the early Indian materials, such as the recent essay by D. D. Kosambi that uses the changes in the productive organization of society as the basis of explanation,[1] or the study by R. Thapar that utilizes the changing forms of political organization to understand the development of early India.[2] Yet to my mind these and similar interpretations are not satisfactory for they assume the primacy of one aspect of society and so organize their explanations of historic change within the whole around change within one part of society. When, for example, there is evidence of a shift in religious or philosophical conception about the eighth century A.D. and no evidence of an earlier change in the social relations associated with the productive process, it is difficult to sustain an explanation of societal change based primarily on the relations of production. Similar problems emerge when the development of society is keyed to changes in forms of political organization. Clearly we need a more capacious explanatory system, one that recognizes the pluralism of economic, political, religious, or social cultures and yet one that relates these cultures into a larger whole, no matter how limited or loosely joined. In this present essay I wish to review a major component of Indian culture, that of communication, which I believe will guide us towards a perception of a central node of culture, if such exists.

In many writers and intellectual traditions there is an appreciation of the centrality of communication in culture. The cultural historian Raymond Williams writes,

> Particular cultures carry particular versions of reality, which they can be said to create, in the sense that cultures carrying different rules (though on a common basis of the evolved human brain) create their own worlds which their bearers only experience. But, further, there is not only variation between cultures, but the individuals who bear these particular cultural rules are capable of altering and extending them, bringing in new or modified rules by which an extended or different reality can be experienced. Thus, new areas of reality can be "revealed" or "created," and these need not be limited to any one individual, but can, in certain interesting ways, be communicated, thus adding to the set of rules carried by the particular culture.[3]

This new reality becomes common to the culture through communication.

In a different manner but with similar perception, the philosopher Ernst Cassirer writes of the system of human activities among which are language, myth, art, science, history, religion—all held together by a common functional bond—the creation of a world of man's own. This created reality is formed through expression and communication.[4] Susanne Langer elaborates Cassirer's views, arguing that the birth of human consciousness comes through the expression of the complex and subtle feelings of the organism in the symbolic form of morality, language, and culture.[5] Common to both positions is the idea that expression and communication form a part of the core of the human consciousness and culture.

From another discipline, anthropology, Clifford Geertz sees

symbolic expression as the principal agency for the creation of culture. Thinking is a social act, a traffic in significant symbols—

> objects in experience (ritual and tools; graven idols and water holes; gestures, markings, images, and sounds) upon which men have impressed meaning. . . . It is through . . . ordered clusters of significant symbols, that man makes sense of the events through which he lives. This study of culture, the accumulated totality of such patterns, is thus the study of the machinery individuals and groups of individuals employ to orient themselves in a world otherwise opaque.[6]

In invoking these names and traditions, I only wish to suggest that the question of the relationship between communication and culture has been perceived as being central to the human experience by diverse thinkers.

This approach to analyzing the Indian data is limited by the nature of the surviving significant symbols. For early India these symbols are restricted to artifactual remains such as pottery, sculpture, temples, or city sites; to certain cultural fossils that are perpetuated in the behavior of the hill tribes or in sacrificial rites, marriage networks, place names, and other such survivals from an earlier time, and finally, to the textual remains. To study the character of communication we can look at the architecture, which may convey through the ornately decorated walls of the temples a sense of magnificence and of the profusion of life, or through the decorated recesses of the cave shrines a retreat from the world or, at a more analytical level, an appreciation of aesthetic organization of space. Obviously any attempt to discern the character of the communication of the ruined architectural remains, or indeed, in any of the surviving examples of the visual arts, is difficult for it requires a rendering into modern systematic communication a message that was conveyed through masses of tiered sculpture or through delicate wall paintings of bygone ages. Yet the difficulties that we can anticipate in understanding and analyzing visual communications pale before the problems involved in trying to read the life style of a contemporary hill tribe of the Shillong plateau or the organization of caste relations and discerning whether they can enable us to understand an earlier phase of human existence in India. Thus while the textual remains are not easy to handle, as will be evident from the shortcomings of this essay, they appear to be by far the most satisfactory of any source for the study of communication and social evolution. Largely concerned with expression, information, and communication, they lead us directly into the question of their function in articulating and creating the culture.

The number and complexity of the texts is so great that the historic corpus must be subdivided for systematic discussion. A useful initial categorization by function is suggested by Jan Vansina, the historian of the Congo, who distinguishes formulae (proverbs, riddles, etc.), poetry, lists of places and persons, narrative tales and commentaries.[7] As these functional types change their character through time we can discern an elementary developmental schema, which groups the texts into three phases. The first is where the texts speak directly and immediately within specific situations. In the earliest phase, as exemplified by the Ṛgveda, the language, on the whole, is concrete and creates a direct impression of color, power, majesty, speed, and so on. Similarly, the early *sūtras* (aphorisms) are very specific. In addition, these first-phase texts are diffuse in their focus, for they appear as collections of poems and wise sayings preserved from earlier times. The systematic ordering of content of information is underdeveloped when contrasted with later materials. For example, the *dharmasūtra* (aphorisms on obligation) topics are not arranged in any systematic fashion while the later *smṛti* (remembered texts) treat their subject consistently under three principal headings—*ācāra* (moral practices), *vyavahāra* (judicial procedures), and *prāyaścitta* (expiation or penance). All we can find is the occasional *manur abravīt* (thus Manu says), a reference to the mythic ancestor of man, parallel to the attribution in modern humor of "Confucius says."

The second-phase texts are functionally more focused, which encouraged the growth of specialized texts with characteristic formats. The complexity and ambiguity of the Ṛgvedic poetry gives way to the expository prose of the Brāhmaṇas describing the details of the sacrificial rites. Secondly, and most obviously, the second-phase texts draw directly on earlier materials, explicating, rationalizing, and expanding the previous teachings.

The third phase of development is indicated by the appearance of systematic, critical, and encyclopaedic texts, many of which are written. It may be exemplified by the philosophical commentaries that build on the Vedic and Brāhmaṇa literature or the legal digests and commentaries that draw together critically the earlier legal literature. During this phase there is further specialization in content, with sophisticated techniques developed to evaluate truth and the authority of divergent texts. There is a corresponding specialization of format leading to further subdivision of the literature.

While we will return to a detailed consideration of these evolutionary phases and their implications for the cultural history of early India, there are two qualifications that must be made. Firstly, that the earlier forms of communication are not replaced or superseded by the later, but rather the earlier and later continue to exist at the same time. Secondly, that while I have treated the evolution of communication as an isolated system, there is good evidence that the array of significant symbols and cultures was heterogeneous and that new inputs were introduced into the system with frequency. For the present I wish to reserve discussion of this heterogeneity

Equipped with these analytical concepts of a formal typology and developmental phases, we can turn to the earliest surviving forms of communication and examine possible cultural correlates. The earliest textual survival is the Ṛgveda *Saṁhitā* which conforms to the poetic type suggested by Vansina. While many of the poems belong to a subtype of religious poetry made up of prayers, hymns, and ritual recitations, there are didactic poems that teach the supreme virtue of charity above all forms of sacrifice. There are also some forty *dānastutis* (praises of giving), which include the famous gambler's lament, which comes close to being a personal poem. There are the dialogue poems of *saṁvādas* such as that between Purūravas and Urvaśī (X.10) or that between Yama and Yamī (X.85). There are the aetiological poems that explain in metaphoric language the forms of creation (X.129), the sacrifice of primal man (*puruṣa*) to sustain creation (X.90), and the hymns to Vāc, who is conceived of as holding together all creation (X.125). But, in addition, there are poems that appear to have been included in the *Saṁhitā* because of their formal aesthetic qualities. It would take too long directly to demonstrate this quality of some of the poems but we might take the concern of one poet for the aptly turned phrase as suggestive of the aesthetic considerations that were important in the compilation.

Quoting from Griffith's archaic translation, part of Hymn 61 of Book I:

> 1. Even to him, swift, strong, and high exalted, I bring my song of praise as dainty viands,
> My thought to him resistless, praise-deserving, prayers offered most especially to Indra.
> 2. Praise like oblation, I present, and utter aloud my song, my fair hymn to the Victor,
> For Indra, who is Lord of old, the singers have decked their lauds with heart and mind and spirit.
> 3. To him then with my lips mine adoration, winning heaven's light, most excellent, I offer,
> To magnify with songs of invocation and with fair hymns the Lord, most bounteous Giver,
> 4. Even for him I frame a laud, as fashions the wright a chariot for the man who needs it,
> Praises to him who gladly hears our praises, a hymn well-formed, all-moving, to wise Indra.
> 5. So with my tongue I deck, to please that Indra, my hymn, as 'twere a horse, through love of glory,
> To reverence the Hero, bounteous Giver, famed far and wide, destroyer of the castles. . . .[8]

The process whereby poems or new information were added cannot be known with certainty, but Louis Renou, who devoted much of his scholarly life to the study of the Veda, suggested that the collection was built up little by little, through selection and retention of the best poems presented in poetic competitions organized by princes or learned groups. These competitions, whose existence is well known in later times, were regulated by a great many conditions and limitations that encouraged the development of an elaborate poetic aesthetic within which the poets sought to outdo each other.[9] The *Sāmhitā* itself "refers to the works of the earlier and later authors [*pūrvaiḥ* and *nūtanaiḥ* (i, 1, 27)], to Agni being worshipped in bygone ages (*pūrve*) by *Ṛṣis* by their hymns (*gīrbhiḥ*) [x, 98, 9] and also to hymns being extemporized for the occasion [*stómaṁ janayāmi návyam* in i, 109, 2, etc.]."[10] New poems were recited and where there were plaudits from the assembly, whether for poetic virtuosity or important concepts, they were incorporated into the collection. Sometime between the eighth and sixth centuries B.C., the corpus that is known to us was closed and few, if any, further poems were added.

Little is known about other types of communication in this earliest phase, though it seems unlikely that poetry was the only form. Recently the development of social aphorisms and formulae into systematic texts has been reviewed by Robert Lingat.[11] He concludes that while no direct information exists about the earliest formulae, these did exist in the earliest times as an amorphous and anonymous body of precepts and adages that were used to guide the resolution of disputes and to encourage moral behavior. These verse precepts or *dharmaśloka*, which were formed as popular and spontaneous expressions, were brought together with other material in the *dharmasūtras* as prose aphorisms. But whether as poetry or in aphoristic prose and poetry they were in a form well suited to memorization and oral reproduction.

As the first-phase communications are all oral, they are entirely dependent upon the retentiveness of the human memory. Thus the poetic and aphoristic prose forms, the metrical and verse organization of the Ṛgveda *Saṁhitā*, as well as the techniques of memorization all served to preserve these early texts. In historic times, the Brahmans are known to have memorized and recited from memory not only the Ṛgveda, but in some instances the whole of the four Vedas. The elaborate mnemonic devices that were devised to assist in accurate recall are well known—such as the *pada-pāṭha* version, where every word element had the euphonic transformations removed and all the compounds were resolved, and the *krama-pāṭha* where every word of the *pada-pāṭha* is pronounced both after the preceding word and before the following word.[12] We also have evidence from other sources of the emphasis on memorization, for the *Mahābhārata* and the *Tantra Vārttika* condemn those who wrote the Vedas and call their knowledge worthless.[13]

There are some obvious inferences from these evidences as to the oral character of the first-phase texts. The information that is communicated only exists in the memory of man. Those who have control over the information are intimately connected with the character of the information they possess. We can reasonably assume that social status is related to the value placed by their society upon the information stored in their memories. A reciprocal relationship probably exists between valued information and high social status. Unless some similar relationship exists, it would be difficult to understand students aspiring to memorize precisely large volumes of material unless there were some obvious rewards. Fortunately, we have in Manu and elsewhere numerous references to both the extended period of strict tutelage and to the highly honored position held by those who successfully mastered the oral texts. The position of the Brāhmana, or information specialist, has been discussed elsewhere, notably in R. K. Mookerji's *Ancient Indian Education.*[14] Suffice it to say that with the standardization of the poetic corpus the place of the creative singer and poet was taken over by the rememberer and priest. The possessor of the technique of recall was honored in place of the singer with his spontaneous art.

Because this information exists only in the memory of man, it is never external to him and can never exist apart from him. Necessarily knowledge has no reified existence or external objectivity. Not that it is subjective as the term is conceived of in popular discourse, but rather that it is held in common in the minds of those who can remember the texts accurately. It can never be examined analytically and critically, as a thing apart, by anyone who has not mastered the text for himself. Further, we might imagine that the effort of recalling accurately required such discipline and concentration that few rememberers could go beyond commenting and elucidating the meaning of the text they had remembered.

A further correlate with the human-centered character of the oral tradition is that the principal orientation of early Indian thought was toward the nature of the human psyche and towards language and communication. It is commonly recognized that the greatest analytical and synthetic achievements were the grammatical studies that were advanced by the concern for the accurate oral reproduction of highly valued texts. Recently a philosopher and student of India, Richard Robinson, reflecting on this achievement, argued that the philosophers used the successful analysis of the grammarians as a model for their philosophical analysis.[15]

> The philosophers quite naturally tried to construct grammars of the world; what holds good for language must hold good for everything, since it is axiomatic that we are to know the unseen from the seen. So they drew up lists of qualitatively distinct elements as observed by common sense and by yogic introspection. Because mental events are especially accessible to this kind of highly trained introspection and because psychology is so much more useful to the yogin than physics, Indian psychology became remarkably sophisticated. This emphasis on linguistics and psychology made Indian philosophy exceptionally anthropocentric; that was in line with the general bias of the civilization. Just as ancient Indian literature treated animals as if they were human beings, just as Indian art treated floral motifs as ornamental adjuncts to human scenes and never developed pure landscape, so Indian philosophy through the ages dwelt on man to the neglect of the rest of existence.[16]

From the surviving literature some guiding conceptions can be inferred. The poetry of the Ṛgveda describes numerous personified energies and anthropomorphic gods who were conceived as acting within the universe in a willful and aggressive manner subject only to an ill-defined overriding law. There is little hierarchy or order, for the gods possess overlapping powers and jurisdictions. When we turn to the form of the collection there is little conceptual unity holding the various hymn cycles together. They stand together because of their formal and substantive similarity and are ordered largely by length and meter rather than by any more general conceptual criteria. From this we might infer only a limited conception for comprehending either society or the forces of the universe.

The character of the information in the Ṛgveda indicates a

society that has not yet begun to value systematic and cumulative information about its own processes and direction, but rather emphasizes the emotional and psychological experience conveyed by the poetic form. Probably it was the sharing of such an experience, rather than in the self-conscious articulation of relations in systematic prose, that Ṛgvedic society achieved its self-identification.

The characteristic feature of the second phase texts is that it elaborates and explicates the earlier material. This rather simple-minded criterion works reasonably well with the Vedic texts and within the *dharmic* tradition that can be taken as illustrative of this phase. Looking first at the *dharma* texts and their development, we can gain some insight into the evolving types of information as well as a particular form which they took. These texts are collections of brief pieces of information designed to assist in the regulation of relations among individuals playing certain roles, families, and groups within the society. As such they fit into Vansina's category of commentaries and mark an elaboration of the earlier legal formulae.[17]

One of the unique features of the *dharma* literature is the explicit concern with the legitimacy of the teachings and the procedures for interpreting and adding new information. Such explicit concern is natural with these texts for their authority derives from their being remembered rather than being heard (*śruti*), as were the Vedas, Brāhmaṇas, and Upaniṣads. The nature of what was being remembered is set out in the *Gautamadharmasūtra* (in I.1–2) and the *Vāsiṣṭhadharmasūtra* (in I.4–6), which state that there are three sources of *dharma*—the *veda*, tradition, and good practices. The reference to the *veda* does not mean the specific *saṁhitās* that are commonly referred to as "Veda," but rather to the whole of knowledge, the sum total of all religious and moral truths perceived by man. Moreover, according to Robert Lingat, the term is extended to include all truths that may be perceived in the future.[18] The other sources of new information are described as being *smṛti*, or the remembered tradition. The term is apparently used in two different senses, for in the earlier *sūtras*, such as that of Gautama, it is those who know the *veda*, also Āpastamba refers to the agreement among those who know the *dharma*,[19] while in some sections of the *Manusmṛti* and for the later śāstric literature generally the term means all of the accepted literature of *dharma-sūtra* and *dharmaśāstra.*[20] There is thus a shift from the accepted tradition being generally characterized as the *veda* to the specification of particular traditions and schools among the interpreters of *dharma.* Clearly, this is a narrowing of the bases of knowledge and a claim to authority by a specialized learned group preserving the traditions of *dharma.* The third source mentioned in the early *sūtras* is the observation of the behavior of good men (*sadācāra* or *śiṣṭa-ācāra*). Lingat warns that this is not to be confused with habitual practices arising from earlier social conventions, but is rather the practices followed generation after generation by those who are at once learned in the Vedas and associated teachings and who are also virtuous. This virtue should guide them in deducing appropriate forms of behavior from the Vedas where the texts themselves are silent on particular problems. In addition to these three sources, which are ranked according to order of appeal, there is a fourth source of *dharma* that is referred to in the later texts as "conscience" (*ātmatuṣṭi*). In the Codes of Manu (XI.12) and Yājñavalkya (I.7) it is stated that when the successive appeal to the *Vedas*, the tradition, and the behavior of virtuous men has failed to provide guidance, then conscience can be consulted. However, not everybody's conscience can be accepted as a guide, but only that of men of great virtue,[21] which brings us close to the observed behavior of good men (*sadācāra*) referred to above. Obviously appeal to any of these authorities individually, and certainly, the successive consultation of all three or four authorities would maintain the possibility of adding new rules, new interpretations, and new information to the corpus of explicitly stated *dharma.*

Unfortunately, among other types of literature characteristic of this phase, such as the Brāhmaṇa literature, there is no modern study of the ways in which new materials might have been added to the corpus of information and I have not found an opportunity to pursue my own inquiries. However, if we accept L. Renou's categorization of the Brāhmaṇas, which is to include not only the Brāhmaṇas themselves but the range of texts explaining and rationalizing the sacrificial acts of the Vedic *saṁhitā*, we can see a progressive textual elaboration that leaves ample opportunity for the incorporation of new information. The texts that Renou grouped with the Brāhmaṇas include sections of the Black *Yajurveda*, the āraṇyakas, the *śrautasūtras* written in the Brāhmaṇa style (such as *Vādhūla*, or portions in that style in such texts as *Baudhāyana*), ritual portions of the great Upaniṣads (the *Bṛhadāraṇyaka* and *Chāndogya*), and the *Jaiminīya-Upaniṣad-Brāhmaṇa*.[22]

These treatises rationalize and explain the sacrificial and ritual activities of the Brahmans. They develop from particular and specific statements about such matters as the movement of the sacrificial cup from east to west, paralleling the movement of the sun, to increasingly general statements about the relationship between man and his universe, the nature of perception, the meaning of the sacrificial act, and other such topics. Within this development from the specific and particular to the general and universal opportunities for interpretation and the addition of new insights were readily available. Moreover, additions to these texts were simplified, for the texts were largely in prose and so alterations were much simpler than with the metrical poems of the *Ṛgveda*. Nor was there the same explicitly stated concern for the word and letter-perfect preservation of the Brāhmaṇa texts that concerned students of the Vedas.

Writing about the development of the various schools of Vedic interpretation in the Brāhmaṇas, R. K. Mookerji suggests that when divergent material had been introduced into the teaching a separate school was frequently formed to perpetuate the modified texts and interpretations. We can imagine, Mookerji writes, that

> a great teacher gathering round him a number of students, introduces to his newly-found colony some sacred texts which differ but slightly from the traditional texts kept up in the community to which he originally belongs. But he himself adds some chapters of his own composition or makes other changes in the imported text which in the eyes of the disciples united under his teachings might be sufficient to constitute a new work that should no longer pass under its original title. Thus new Charaṇas [Vedic schools] would be founded. . . .[23]

Such speculative reconstructions of the process whereby variations in the information were added to the existing texts gains some support from the later tradition surrounding the formation of the Navadvīpa center for teaching of logic by Vāsudeva Sārvabhauma. Upon completing his studies in Benares during the latter part of the fifteenth century, he journeyed to Mithila, the foremost center for logical studies. As a condition for being accepted as a student, he had to promise not to transcribe the manuscript of the *Tattvacintāmaṇi*, the principal treatise on logic, which was held as a private monopoly by the Mithila school. However, Vāsudeva, adhering to the terms of his promise, if not to the spirit, memorized the text together with the commentaries of the Mithila teachers and parts of other texts, and moved to Navadvīpa where he founded the school of logic that was to supplant Mithila in preeminence.[24] For our present illustration it is revelant that the Mithila teachers, while relying on the texts of *Tattvacintāmaṇi*, had developed commentaries elucidating and expanding the study of logic as did Vāsudeva when he began teaching at Navadvīpa. It is likely that a similar process occurred in earlier times. The process of adding new information seems plausible, if not always well documented. Moreover, it is clear that the development of new teachings led to specialized forms of information.

Among the specialized forms are those developed to preserve the accuracy of the Vedic *saṁhitās*. The earliest reference to these occurs in the *Muṇḍaka Upaniṣad* (I.1.5) which is dated between 500–200 B.C.[25] The *Muṇḍaka* refers to pronunciation (*śikṣā*), ritual (*kalpa*), grammar (*vyākaraṇa*), definition or vocabulary (*nirukta*), metrics (*chandas*), and astrology (*jyotiṣa*) as auxiliary disciplines to be cultivated by the student of the Vedas. A similar process of specialization may be seen in the development of the various *caraṇas* of the Brāhmaṇas that were referred to earlier. Also in this phase the distinction emerges between the *śrautasūtra*, *gṛhyasūtra*, and *dharmasūtra*, and the bases of *vedāntasūtra* and *yogasūtra* were probably laid.

As new information is related to specialization, so does it correlate with the new forms of textual organization that were not provided for in Vansina's typology. While poetry and aphorism continue, the explanatory prose format is used in the Brāhmaṇa texts and the dialogue form of question and answer appears frequently in the Upaniṣads, as may be illustrated by the exchanges between Yājñavalkya and his questioners in the *Bṛhadāraṇyaka Upaniṣad.*[26] The formats reflect not only the shift in the nature of the information, but also in the role of the information specialist. The expression is that of a declarative authority or a teacher, rather than the oracular statement of the wise sage or the emotionally more complex and semantically ambiguous hymn of the poet. The expository and teaching function has become paramount in this type of communication. With the development of different traditions as well as the prose style in which the traditions were expressed, it seems highly probable that the emphasis on memorization declined, relatively, and more attention was devoted to a discussion and understanding of the significance of the texts.

The concern with the comprehension of concepts occurred at a time when writing probably began to be used for storing and recalling information. There is no direct survival of written materials until the fourth century B.C. and the earliest corpus is the inscriptions of Aśoka (ca. 264 B.C.). Nonetheless, the circumstantial evidence of the use of writing carries some weight. We know that writing was in use in the merchant communities of western and central Asia by the ninth century B.C. and that Indian merchants were in contact with these traders. Secondly, the teachings of Pāṇini (4th century B.C.) may assume the existence of an alphabet. Thirdly, the earliest examples of writing show a well-developed and standardized script form in the Brahmi alphabet with a variant form in the northwest that is related to the alphabets of western Asia. For these reasons I am inclined to think that the technique of writing was known and that it was used to record teachings and important doctrines that were couched in the increasingly common prose style. If we can rely on the story of the way in which the manuscript of *Tattvacintāmaṇi* was used as a basic resource in the Mithila school of logic and how the monopoly of this teaching was broken when Vāsudeva Sārvabhauma memorized the teaching, then we may have some insight into the manner in which writing was used within the learned community. Written texts were probably used as a repository of information to which the teacher would refer privately, to assist in the instruction of his students.

The changing form and substance of information as well as the changes in the character of the information specialist and the techniques of storing and recalling information have wide-ranging implications of which only a few can be briefly mentioned here. One of the most obvious implications is that as information increases in volume and becomes differentiated, and as the energy and skills required for mastering any segment become greater, specialization occurs among the information specialists. This leads in turn to professionalism, with gratuities and endowments being set aside to support different specialized groups such as priests, teachers, judges, doctors, and the like. The variety of forms of information with associated specialists encourages the development of hierarchic society where social gradations are worked out among the professional information specialists, and between the specialists, their patrons and protectors, and the rest of society. The political organization of a hierarchic society is clearly a concern of the *dharmasūtras* and is elaborated in great detail in the *dharmaśāstras*. Kingship is assumed to be the natural form of political organization. Suggestive parallels thus exist between the increasingly systematic and formalized information and the formalization of social and political relations. Religious thought tends in the same direction, for the large number of separately named anthropomorphic forces with overlapping jurisdictions found in the Ṛgveda became, in the Upaniṣads, subsumed into the universal cosmic spirit, *Brahman*. The concurrent concern for the individual's position in society and his moral responsibility probably encouraged the doctrine of the transmigrating moral entity. "Moral individualism thus appears as an extension of social individualism, and the transmigrant person is a moral counterpart of the legal person."[27] Types of information, social and political organization, and religious concept mark an evolution in the direction of a more differentiated, individualized, and hierarchic society and the elaboration of ways of conceiving of the relations between the parts and the whole.

The third developmental phase of information is not marked by a distinctive shift in form or in technique of storing and recalling information. Earlier tendencies are further elaborated with the multiplication of specialized forms of information; with the development of more objective and systematic means of generating and incorporating new information into the corpus of accepted teachings, and with a pronounced tendency towards encyclopaedism and a correlative move towards higher levels of abstraction. There is the accumulation and long-term storage of information in areas of activity that were hitherto neglected. One finds the emergence of a self-awareness about information, its societal significance, and an enhanced consciousness of a cultural unity. There are other qualitative changes that we might have considered but for the present I would suggest that the increase in quantity is of a sufficient order to justify making a distinction between the second phase and this last phase.

Illustrating these developments are the legal commentaries and digests as well as the philosophical commentaries. The *dharma* texts fall into two categories: the commentaries (*bhāṣya, vṛtti, vyākhyā, vivaraṇa*) that elaborate and explicate a particular *smṛti* text, and the digests or treatises (*nibandha*) that treat the whole of the legal literature or marshal previous discussions on one branch of legal lore. However, both groups of texts are markedly different from the earlier *dharmaśāstras*, for they are primarily concerned with simplifying, clarifying, and reconciling contradictory injunctions. These third-phase texts are much more complex, both because of their length and scope and because of their internal organization. The *Kṛtyakalpataru* of Lakṣmīdhara (first minister of Govindacandra, king of Kanauj, 1104–54 A.D., comprises some 30,000 *ślokas* or roughly one-third of the length of the Mahābhārata. Where the earlier *Yājñavalkyasmṛti* followed a simple tripartite division into *ācāra, vyavahāra*, and *prāyaścitta*, the *Kṛtyakalpataru* is divided into fourteen sections, which treat of many additional subjects. For example the earlier category of *vyavahāra* is now divided into two separate sections—*vyavahāra* proper (a discussion of the composition of courts of justice and of judicial procedures) and *vivāda*, which discusses eighteen forms of litigation.[28] Moreover there is a development of a technical vocabulary in the *dharma* texts with terms being standardized for various legal relations, functions of the court, gradations of liability, until the legal lexicon became as fully complex as our own.

Similar observations might be made about the philosophical texts. The philosophical thought found in the Upaniṣads is refined and elaborated in the *ṣaḍdarśana*, the six classical Hindu systems of philosophy: *nyāya* or analysis, *vaiśeṣika* or individual characteristics, *sāṅkhya* or enumerating, *yoga* or discipline, *mīmāṃsā* or inquiry, and *uttara mīmāṃsā* or *vedānta*. In the philosophical commentaries, truth tests were devised and an analytical and logical rigor was applied to developing the coherence and power of each system. Exponents of the various traditions engaged in lengthy and intellectually taxing controversy that constantly challenged the adequacy of the teachings. As the old system was modified, new schools sprang up, as illustrated by the Navadvīpa school of logic or *Navyanyāya*, which we have referred to earlier, gaining preeminence over other schools by its analytical and argumentative power. Much remains to be said but it is more interesting to turn to some implications of the third-phase texts and then to a reconsideration of the whole developing system of information.

The characterization of the information specialist shifts away from poet and the priest-teacher towards what, for want of inspiration, I call the organization expert. The appearance in the historical sources of administrators who command a range of technical, legal, and governmental information and the philosopher who develops his teachings to serve a particular monastic order is illustrative. Recall as examples Lakṣmīdhara, the author of the *Kṛtyakalpataru* and the first minister to Govindacandra, ruler of Kanauj; Aparāka, himself king of Koṅkan (1110–40), who commented on the *Yājñavalkyasmṛti*; Hemādri, a minister of Mahādeva (1260–73) of the Yādava dynasty, who wrote the immense treatise entitled *Caturvargacintāmaṇi*; or Śaṅkarācārya (ca. 788–820), the famed commentator on the *Brahmasūtra* of Bādarāyaṇa, who is reported to have been the founder of a monastic order to advance his Vedāntic teaching.

Another implication of this shift is the reciprocal relation between the information needed to guide the operation of organizations becoming more voluminous, complex, and spanning longer time, and the organizations themselves expanding, developing long-term goals, and mobilizing greater resources to achieve their more ambitious goals. In the political organizations the number of administrative offices itemized in the historical inscriptions increase in number, while in the texts references to scribes and other record keepers multiply. Religious organizations become more complex, as witness the elaboration of Buddhist monasticism that developed from a band of adherents who sheltered together during the rainy season into immense establishments administering endowments, libraries, shrines, teaching programs, and so on. Obviously as the organizations expand their functions it is no longer possible for them to be guided solely by common sense, conventional wisdom, or divine inspiration. The dynamics of expanding organizations and the development of specialized and technical information enhances the role of the information specialist and, conversely, the existence of the organization expert makes possible these other developments.

The general character of the change may be summed up as an intensification of the process of specialization and a multiplication of hierarchic relations with a corresponding diminution in the coherence of society. While numerous subdivisions within society are described and minutely prescribed, new organizational forms such as the long-lived governmental administrations, monastic orders, temple-centered religious organizations, merchant guilds, all of which are referred to in the inscriptions, stand outside any known attempt to conceive of the whole of the society. Clearly no single agency commanded the conceptual or executive capacity to comprehend the whole of society. Pluralistic hierarchies of specialized information were matched by pluralistic organizational hierarchies. Notwithstanding the efforts of the encyclopaedists to organize all information, the complexity of society defied effective ordering and centralization. Regional and local centers of political power grew in relative significance as earlier imperial forms collapsed or otherwise fell into desuetude. Religious sects appear in the records with the *bhakti* movement and its manifestations in the Bhāgavata, Pāñcarātra, Pāśupata, and Āgamic Śaivite literature, as well as Śāktas, Jains, Buddhists, and their variants. In short, there had emerged in early India complex, parallel, and competing information systems with a correlative change in the political and religious cultures.

We have now briefly sketched three possible phases in the development of information and suggested how the characteristic form and substance of those surviving remains might be used to locate and examine the historical evolution of some central core of Indian culture. In this preliminary essay I do not wish to suggest that the three phases outlined above represent anything more than an initial schema, which will be subsequently refined. The millenial leaps, from the first phase falling prior to the eighth century B.C., the second phase lasting until approximately the fourth century, A.D., with the third phase terminating in the fourteenth century, is clearly a very coarse-grained sieve for sorting the surviving sources of information. But while this preliminary survey is crude, I do think that the study of the organization of information and communication is a most promising approach to the location of a variable, central to the early culture of India. A demonstration of this contention must await the completion of the more extensive and carefully documented study upon which I am presently engaged.

Addendum

I wish to thank Burton Stein, Edwin Pulleyblank, Ashok Aklujkar, and Marc Beach for their criticism of an earlier version of this paper. While I have accepted many of their comments two major differences remain. Firstly, I would argue that the analysis of information and communication is not simply an index to more profound changes in society or, alternatively, a variant rationalization of the surviving data, but is at the very nexus of human culture. Secondly, I think all historians engage in sociologizing—that is, applying regularities perceived in one context to the explanation of relations elsewhere. Where the difference seems to lie between us is whether large-scale regularities exist, or can be adequately perceived, and whether once perceived they can be used to explain relations within different kinds of systems or, in this case, societies. This question can be resolved in the affirmative only by a number of demonstrations. It is a task crucial for the foundations of cultural history.

NOTES

1. D. D. Kosambi, *Ancient India* (New York: Pantheon Books, 1965).
2. R. Thapar, *A History of India*, 2 vols. (London: Penguin Books, 1966), vol. 1.
3. Raymond Williams, *The Long Revolution* (New York: Harper Torchbooks, 1966), p. 18.
4. Ernst Cassirer, *An Essay on Man* (New Haven: Yale University Press, 1962), p. 68 ff.
5. Susanne K. Langer, *Mind: An Essay on Human Feeling* (Baltimore: The Johns Hopkins Press, 1967).

6. Clifford Geertz, *Person, Time, and Conduct in Bali: An Essay in Cultural Analysis,* Southeast Asia Studies (New Haven: Yale University Press, 1966), pp. 4–5.

7. Jan Vansina, *Oral Tradition: A Study in Historical Methodology* (Chicago: Aldine Publishing Company, 1965), pp. 146–60.

8. Ralph T. H. Griffith, trans., *The Hymns of the Ṛgveda* (Varanasi: The Chowkhamba Sanskrit Series, vol. 35, 1963), pp. 82–83.

9. L. Renou, *Histoire de la Langue Sanskrite* (Lyon: Editions IAC, 1956), p. 11.

10. Quotation includes material in square brackets. R. K. Mookerji, *Ancient Indian Education* (Delhi: Motilal Banarsidass, 1960), p. 18.

11. Robert Lingat, *Les Sources du Droit dans le Système Traditionnel de l'Inde* (Paris: Mouton and Co., 1967).

12. Mookerji, *Ancient Indian Education*, p. 21.

13. Ibid., p. 27.

14. Ibid., p. 5 ff.

15. See also J. F. Staal, "Philosophy and Language," in *Essays in Philosophy.* Presented to Dr. [T. M. P.] Mahadevan (Madras, 1962), pp. 10–25.

16. Richard H. Robinson, "Classical Indian Philosophy," mimeographed (Madison, Wis., n.d.), pt. 1, p. 153.

17. Vansina, *Oral Tradition*, pp. 160–61.

18. Lingat, *Sources du Droit dans le Système Traditionnel*, p. 22.

19. Ibid., p. 27.

20. Ibid., p. 28.

21. Ibid., p. 20.

22. L. Renou's preface to Sylvain Lévi, *La Doctrine du Sacrifice dans les Brâhmaṇas*, 2d ed. (Paris: Presses Universitaires de France, 1966), note pp. vii–viii.

23. Mookerji, *Ancient Indian Education,* pp. 81–82.

24. Ibid., p. 217.

25. J. N. Farquhar, *An Outline of the Religious Literature of India* (Delhi: Motilal Banarsidass, 1967), p. 58.

26. R. E. Hume, *The Thirteen Principal Upanishads,* 2d ed. (London: Oxford University Press, 1931), pp. 107–26.

27. Robinson, "Classical Indian Philosophy," pp. 178–79.

28. Lingat, *Sources du Droit dans le Système Traditionnel*, p. 129.

Some Thoughts on Indian Government Policy as it Affects Sanskrit Education

Edwin Gerow

श्रीः The position of Sanskrit education in the modern Indian State is anomalous to an unmatched degree. Historically, the Sanskrit school reflects values in which caste and religious preoccupations predominate. The system of education articulates those values in their most sophisticated form. Yet, because it is an *educational* system (as functionally opposed to a less easily defined confessional or religious one) it finds itself in principle under the jurisdiction of the officially secular state—unlike the *devasthāna*, the *maṭha* and similar institutions, which, though regulated, are still considered private. Most of the important Sanskrit colleges, like Mahārāja's Sanskrit College, Mysore, are now directly administered by state or national educational bureaucracies.[1] Those many local colleges that remain *de jure* under the government of religious bodies[2] are subjected to state control at their two most vital points: all receive a subvention from the state based on enrollment and other factors; and all, in fact, do train students for the officially administered state-wide Sanskrit examinations.

Local and State Control—Some Exceptions

Yet these colleges—run under the auspices, and usually within the precincts of a religious endowment, constitute the only significant exception to the pattern of growing secular control—

insofar as they accept advanced students.

For such students are being trained (in our terms) as theologians, committed to the particular branch of philosophy (vedānta) patronized by the endowment, under, in the typical case, the direct guidance of the superior (*svāmi*) of the *maṭha* (particularly if he is a scholar himself). The lives of these students will be spent in the service of the *svāmi* and the *maṭha*, in defending the faith publicly, serving as authority in the many ritual disputes and difficulties that are part of the *maṭha*'s ongoing routine. They thus escape the secularism that is elsewhere dominant in the system. Associated with the Śaṃkarācārya of Śṛṅgeri[3] are several families whose tradition has been to train their sons in such service: not only in Advaita, but even in particular disciplines where expertise was necessary to the *maṭha* authorities: *nyāya* (logic) and *mīmāṃsā* (semantics of ritual activity). H.H. the Pejāvaramaṭha *svāmi*, one of the eight who, like a college of equal popes, govern the chief shrine of the Mādhva branch of Vedānta in Uḍupi, has founded a college in Bangalore, which, though it does train students for the public Sanskrit examinations, is primarily intended to educate young Mādhva boys in their *saṃpradāya*, and in the logic of disputation, so necessary in confronting other Vedānta scholars and systems. The graduates of this twelve-year school are assured by H.H. the *svāmi* of a lifetime subvention that assures also their adhesion to the faith, and their attendance if need be upon the person and the projects of the *svāmi*. Such educational enterprises are possible only within those orthodox orders that are wealthy and enlightened enough to respond to the problems that are implied by increasing state control of the Sanskritic educational system. Pejāvara himself, a vivacious, humble, sophisticated, and learned young man, enjoys great authority among his devotees. He has consistently found support for his undertakings in pursuit of traditional excellence. It is not far from the truth to say that he and men like him represent the hope of Sanskrit study in Mysore State —insofar as traditional values are considered fundamental to it.

Even for the maintainance and repair of Sanskrit schools attached to *maṭhas*, the *maṭha* authorities are often obliged to turn to the Muzrai Board.[4] The lamentable condition of the Sanskrit college in Melukoṭe is proof of how little money is available for such purposes. This college—the oldest in all South India—is said to be one of two founded by the East India Company directly.[5] Melukoṭe, the Śrīvaiṣṇava center in Mysore—where Rāmānuja himself spent fourteen years of his exile and won many disciples to his new philosophy—even Melukoṭe can pay its principal no more than 100 rupees per month ($13). Its buildings I found in disrepair. In a narrow, windowless room, for years without whitewash, a few Brahman boys seated on the floor earnestly recited the *Amarakośa*. The only light came from the open door and from holes in the roof—the light of God, as I was told. I understood then why the school generally took its holidays during the rainy season.

The Pattern of Local Secular Control: The Problem of Orthodoxy

The secularization of Sanskrit education—understood as a life-style—is indeed a contradiction in terms, and yet it is the official policy of all governmental bodies concerned with Sanskrit education. In the context of this confrontation the question of the survival of the Sanskrit school is now debated. Two positions are taken—themselves defining the dilemma:

a) Sanskrit education cannot survive shorn of its traditional religious functions and support.
b) Sanskrit education can survive only if secularized and introduced into the mainstream of Indian life.

The solution as we see it must somehow bridge the horns of this dilemma.

Soon after Independence, Mahārāja's Sanskrit College (MSC), which had formerly been an all-Brahman school by royal decree, was opened to all castes, and teaching posts were filled without regard to orthodox notions of purity (*śuddhi*). In a context in which Sanskrit education is declining, this has accomplished little more than to demoralize the orthodox. It is rare enough to see even a Brahman today seriously undertake Vedic study or medieval logic or grammar.[6] The only groups to take effective advantage of the opening of Sanskrit institutions have been those other high castes who define their social status in terms of spiritual authority similar to that of the Brahman. It is not clear that these castes were ever systematically excluded.[7] In Mysore the chief beneficiaries[8] have been the Vīraśaiva community, which has evolved a caste order duplicating in orthodoxy the Brahmanical (even to an authoritative commentary on the Vedānta *sūtras*), and many of whom were, it is thought, converted from Brahmans anyway. For centuries the Liṅgāyat *gurus* had themselves studied Sanskrit and established training for their adepts in certain branches of Sanskrit learning. Despite this functional equivalence, the Brahman castes had generally been considered the exclusive arbiter of the sanctum sanctorum itself, the Veda. This exclusivity in Mysore was reflected in policies and restrictions of the royal government, especially as Sanskrit colleges were concerned with matters Vedic. Now Government has adopted the contrary position: even the Vedic sections are in principle open to all castes.

But of course *Veda* is more than the book itself or even its recitation. In earlier years, before Independence, the life of students and teachers in MSC was conducted according to the Vedic prescriptions concerning study. The royal government had repeatedly affirmed the school's special status in this respect.[9] One did not hear, nor teach Sanskrit (considered Veda or Vedāṅga) unless one were in a state of *śuddhi* (Kan.: *maḍi*)—ritual purity, assured by ritual bathings, and worship, wearing a clean cloth, recitation of the *saṃdhyāvandana*, and abstinence from certain polluting acts, such as eating, or commerce with those not so purified. Respect for these principles, and not the notion that Sanskrit itself was incommunicable, had made the traditional teacher reluctant to share his Sanskrit, however "secular" the subject, with the ritually impure. Opening the colleges to those who are unwilling or unable to observe the principle of *śuddhi* has struck at the very heart of the orthodox teacher's or student's caste *dharma*. Most students, and some teachers, have responded simply by abandoning pretense to purity, attributing their sense of guilt to *kaliyuga*. Many teachers, who would otherwise prefer to do so, cannot withdraw from the college (though some did, in response to the democratization of Vedic study) for their only source of income is a professorship. Others maintain their purity, but in a manner liminary to the college: sometimes taking serious students to their homes.

We should emphasize that it was not Sanskrit itself that the orthodox believed to be their prerogative: it was not the subject matter as such (except for Veda) that was reserved, rather it was the method and the context of study, determined according to the precedents of tradition, that made the *activity* of learning improper in the presence of those not similarly consecrated. That Sanskrit was known and appreciated by others, for example westerners, was generally praised by orthodox scholars (provided the opportunities for orthodoxy were not thereby restricted).[10] Sanskritic subjects have always been classified into "sacred" and "profane" (*vaidika* and *laukika*) by the orthodox, and it has long been traditional for high-caste non-Brahmans to undertake such study under the guidance of a Brahman teacher.[11] While visiting a Jain school in an *āśrama* in Shimoga District, I was introduced to the two Sanskrit teachers—both were North Indian Brahmans—one from Orissa, a center of orthodoxy. Such relationships are clearly approved by the tradition, even where "non-Hindus" are concerned.

About one-third of the students in MSC and a smaller proportion of teachers are now Liṅgāyats. Most appear less orthodox than their Brahman colleagues. But orthodoxy is hardly an issue—and many Brahmans are far from orthodox—for no standards of *śuddhi* are enforced. Inevitably, the admission of Liṅgāyat students and teachers, and a few other students (in the primary grades), is interpreted by most Brahman teachers as an indication of the general relapse of standards. It is clear that this is the case not because Liṅgāyats are now admitted, but because the state has withdrawn its sanction of that orthodoxy that—among others—the Liṅgāyats themselves would like to see strengthened. The state's interest appears only to achieve a certain mathematical "parity" in employment and admission, without reference to any set of standards: this alone would suffice to demoralize a qualified orthodox teacher—be he Brahman or Liṅgāyat. It is—alas!—reasonably clear that the college will have ceased to function effectively, long before "parity" is reached.

The state is consciously attempting to "secularize" ("popularize") Sanskritic education—at a time when few students (even among the most orthodox) would consider taking up the traditional study of Sanskrit. Since Independence, not a single non-Brahman and non-Liṅgāyat student has passed through MSC to a degree. Further, only *one* of the approximately 150 registered Liṅgāyat students now in MSC is devoting himself exclusively to Sanskrit at the *Vidvat* level (he is a Liṅgāyat *guru*); and fewer than 30 of the 250 Brahman boys fall in this class. A few modern subjects have been introduced in the curriculum—but fewer in Mysore than almost anywhere else in India.[12] The urge to modernize curriculum originates at the Centre, as an aspect of the Centre's official policy to support and preserve Sanskrit study.[13] But at the state level secularization and democracy are understood still in largely caste-oriented terms: modernization becomes a part of the hostility to Brahmanism, which for various reasons (not all having to do with orthodoxy)—is general in the south anyway. Thus "modernization" is less a movement from East to West than a shift in authority among "traditional" groups. Left to themselves, the orthodox would contrive somehow to preserve their educational culture, but they are not being permitted to do so and no alternatives are available.

We must add the important proviso that the *institution* described here as "traditional" is in fact quite modern: the "college" in which these orthodox practices were maintained integrally until 1947, is qua institution modern —dating from 1868—for which earlier parallels are wanting. It is clear, not only that the college was established as a response to the Western type of educational institution then in process of foundation in India, but that those who established the college (H. H. Kṛṣṇarāja Wodeyar, Divan Rangacharlu) saw it as a new state-supported and centralized organization of modes of study that traditionally had been dispersed and local, largely under the direct control of individual teachers, learned *ācāryas*. In this perspective, the maintenance of Vedic prescriptions of study in the college represented in part an effort to impose on a modern institution styles of learning that were not pertinent to it; their abandonment in 1947 can be seen in institutional terms as the admission that that effort to re-traditionalize was misdirected. By this argument the apparent retreat from orthodoxy in 1947, however great its psychological impact, is much muted in its significance.

The state of Mysore (like other states in the Indian Union) is the chief monetary support of Sanskrit study. The major colleges are state-maintained, students receive state stipends; private Sanskrit schools receive yearly grants (based on the number of students), which alone, in most cases, allow them to exist. It is not therefore correct to imply that the state is uniquely responsible for the decline that affects Sanskrit study. Still, these funding policies in Mysore are extensions of provisions made during the

Mahārāja's rule, and represent, in these very different circumstances, more toleration than encouragement. We must note, however, one measure that the state of Mysore has independently taken: as an extension of the scheme of subventions to private schools, and possibly to encourage education in those remote areas not served by even a government primary school, individual teachers have been awarded subventions in lieu of salary, provided at least six of their students appear for (not "pass") the *prathamā* or elementary Sanskrit examination yearly (taken about age 10). Because of this measure, a significant *increase* has been noted recently in small Sanskrit (ordinarily one-teacher) schools, not only in the rural areas but in the larger cities as well.[14] In effect, this state policy has encouraged, not Sanskrit study, per se, but rather a return at the elementary level to the condition of Sanskrit study before the establishment of the great colleges in the nineteenth century. Most of the teachers to take advantage of the subvention are Brahman.

In other states, conditions vary dramatically. A conclusion that paradoxically emerges from this study done chiefly in Mysore is that the subject of Sanskrit education cannot be easily generalized and must be taken up on a state-by-state basis. From very limited exposure or even hearsay (newspaper accounts and the like), it became obvious that the condition of Sanskrit very much depended on the toleration level it enjoyed in its local environment. Its "decline" being much a function of local conditions was thus hardly a decline at all, but a set of often divergent responses to pressures themselves inconsistent. In Madras, conditions are now far worse than in Mysore, despite, in the recent past, one of the most brilliant local reputations in the entire subcontinent. In Uttar Pradesh, the heart of Āryāvarta, where Sanskrit is officially encouraged, and the only independent Sanskrit *university* has been established, many respected senior pundits are Madrassis—a situation that cannot recur, not only because there are no Madrassi pundits being trained, but also because teacher recruitment has become an increasingly local, as opposed to national, phenomenon. In Gujarat, the chief Sanskrit college is a functional part of Baroda University, and enjoys parity in those terms. The director remains correspondingly optimistic about placing his students in respectable careers. In Orissa, the new conservative state ministry (Jana

Sangha and former Princes' coalition) has taken steps (newspaper account, 1968) to establish new Sanskrit colleges in districts where there were none, and to require Sanskrit as a second language in all high schools. Across India, the prospects for Sanskrit appear as varied as the local conditions and the local politics.

National Policy and Sanskrit Education: The Problem of Employment

Still, on a pan-Indian basis, the condition of Sanskrit education, though in some places appearing more desperate than in others, is nowhere more than dreary.[15] And this is not surprising, for national policy itself has played and continues to play a crucial role in determining the prospects for Sanskrit study. While the central government exercises no direct administrative control over education, it wields potent influence. The University Grants Commission analogy for the universities illustrates the effective limits imposed by the Centre on the pro forma local autonomy of the states.

In explicit terms the interest of the Centre has been expressed (however timidly) exclusively in support of traditional Sanskrit study, notably in constituting and in implementing partially the recommendations of the Sanskrit Commission (1956–57). The monumental *Report* of the Sanskrit Commission (published 1958) bears witness in eloquent and starkly realistic terms to the conditions of Sanskrit education, and formulates a measured program of responsibilities for the Centre in encouragement thereof.[16] A bureau, the Central Sanskrit Board, has been established within the Ministry of Education to advise the minister and discharge policies. A number of national fellowships have been established. National Sanskrit competitions and prizes have been inaugurated, and carry handsome honoraria (in the pundit's world). The chief initiative of the Centre, however, has been in maintaining a Sanskrit university (in Benares), which has pro forma parity with other Indian universities, even at the postgraduate level. The Vārāṇaseya Saṃskṛta Viśvavidyālaya was not founded by the Centre[17] but through the initiative of Dr. Sampurnand, Uttar Pradesh chief minister; it now enjoys official protection. At least two *Kendriyavidyāpīṭhas* have been established (Delhi, Tirupati),[18] not so much to teach, as to teach traditional teachers how to teach in high schools. A program recommending modernization of the Sanskrit curriculum is also being prepared at the present time by the Central Sanskrit Board.[19]

Still, these encouragements on the part of the Centre, laudable and effective as they undoubtedly are, do not respond to the fundamental problems facing Sanskrit education today. The influence of the Centre on Sanskrit education is seen less in overt and explicit encouragement than in accidental redundance of policies intended to have their chief effect in fields far removed from Sanskrit, but which to a large degree determine the provision of a reasonable livelihood for the graduates of the traditional system. Though the Sanskrit Commission did not face this question squarely, it is clear, had their major recommendations been implemented, that the problem would not have assumed the disastrous proportions we see today. Chiefly, the commission saw the employment opportunities for pundits very much in terms of the status quo, where the pundit was essentially a teacher of Sanskrit language and culture, and sought to guarantee economic viability to the *śāstraic* graduate (1) by requiring Sanskrit as a compulsory subject for most if not all Hindu high-school students,[20] and (2) by assuring parity in employment and other areas between traditional and Western (university) Sanskrit graduates.[21]

These core recommendations have not been implemented; moreover, two initiatives of the Centre, unrelated to Sanskrit per se, have further compromised the prospects of employment for the traditional graduate, and thus have sapped the remaining vitality of the traditional system. The two measures amount to unintentional repudiations of the recommendations of the Sanskrit Commission. Both are attempts to deal with problems facing a new, strikingly diverse nation committed to modernization and secularization. The best known is the three-language formula. Under British rule, Sanskrit enjoyed a privileged status in every government high school—where most students were upper-caste. It was one of the optional required second languages (English being required of all students) which in effect was taken by all Brahman boys and by most Hindus throughout their secondary school career. The vernaculars did not as a rule enjoy comparable administrative support, though of course they could be studied.

The British-patronized renascence in Sanskrit during the nineteenth and early twentieth century was largely due to the effective grafting of traditional Sanskrit study onto the so-called modern educational system, not only in founding *colleges* for the study of Sanskrit, but by giving great encouragement to graduates of traditional colleges, who alone, it was generally thought, were qualified to teach Sanskrit, even in the newer or Western schools.

Since Independence this situation has changed. The vernacular language of the region and the new national language have both been elevated over Sanskrit in high-school curriculum priority, reducing Sanskrit to the status of a fourth language, which few students have time to study and fewer schools can afford to staff. Since teaching is the chief career for students of Sanskrit, the result has been a decline in the number of positions available to the graduates of traditional institutions, and an increasingly moribund condition in the latter as their own students decline in numbers and quality.

It is often maintained in other contexts by central and state authorities that the Sanskrit degrees are "equivalent" to B.A., M.A. or even (in the case of Vārāṇaseya Saṃskṛta Viśvavidyālaya) to the Ph.D. What this means is far from clear for unless such qualificatory discriminations are removed, the degrees will not be *operationally* equivalent.[22]

At the same time, partly in response to the favors shown the Western degrees, it is generally believed that a B.A. or an M.A. in Sanskrit has a better chance of employment than the traditional Sanskrit graduate even in the field of Sanskrit teaching. The few positions that remain in the secondary schools are often awarded to the B.A. in preference to the pundit, which further diminishes the latter's hopes of employment. It is often said that the B.A. or M.A. can teach modern subjects besides Sanskrit, while the pundit cannot. Since Sanskrit teaching is rarely a full-time occupation now, this argument carries weight in the smaller schools. In effect, the prospects of the pundit are reduced to those rare positions where his real expertise is an absolute necessity: staffing the Sanskrit colleges themselves, or as research assistants to the Western-trained professor of Sanskrit in a university or Oriental research facility. But even pundits for these positions are not being trained. Few men will spend twelve or more years arduously preparing themselves for a livelihood that is not apt to provide clothes or sustenance for their children. The pundit's devotion to *dharma* is limited by universal economic laws.

Respect for the traditional degree has also been diminished by the second of the two governmental initiatives mentioned. In 1956 a directive was issued to improve the educational qualifications of higher rank civil servants: no applicant could be admitted to the examinations for those ranks who lacked the B.A. or M.A. from an approved university.[23] There appears to have been no consideration of its consequences for the holders of traditional degrees. Though few would normally seek higher civil service positions (Indian Administrative Services, etc.), it is still true that the prejudicially low ceiling in pay and advancement thus imposed on the non-Western degree holder constitutes an effective restraint on ambition, and appears to canonize administratively the prejudice felt in many sectors of Indian public life favoring the M.A. or B.A. graduate.

A university teaching post—even in a Department of Sanskrit! —is now in practical terms unavailable to the holder of a Sanskritic degree—so exclusive have the qualificatory rules become in the universities. The great Indian Sanskritists of the past (and even to some extent of the present) were generally men who excelled in both their own traditional cultural forms and in Western ones. Not only is this admirable blending of cultures not recognized as an ideal, but it is now increasingly difficult for even determined men to pursue both trainings. In this area the Sanskrit Commission appeared to see the chief problem as the premature fusing of the two systems, but the reverse appears to be the case:[24] the two systems increasingly accept only students who have passed antecedent examinations within their own system—demonstrating the principle that all bureaucracies become self validating. The loss to the traditional system is certainly great. But the loss to the modern system, in the fields of Sanskrit and Indian history and culture, is incalculable and should be recognized as a national problem in its own right. *Both* systems are becoming moribund from their artificial separation—a condition certainly never envisaged by those who set up Western-style degree programs in the last century. Now it will soon be the case that foreign Sanskritists will know Sanskrit better than Indians themselves, for they are more and more committed to the study of Sanskrit as a *cultural* medium.

The effect of these rules, together with the three-language

formula, has been to demoralize those very circles whose social function, and whose self-awareness, prepare them to perpetuate the best of the Indian classical tradition as it has been entrusted to the present generation of men.

The Indian secular state appears to be at war with its own past—a real past—one held in deep respect, if not in awe, by humanists of every nation. Many developing countries are engaged in recreating a past out of nothing; the Indian nation seems more concerned with the opposite, oppressed as it is with its past, apparently more glorious than its present—or its prospects of the future. No serious case can be made against Sanskrit study: in political terms the great tradition of Indian civilization is the single most important unifying force in India today; the existence of a corps of cultural specialists devoted to its perpetuation, without whom the very tradition would collapse for want of skill (so interrelated are the substance of the tradition and its modes of perpetuation), is certainly highly desirable. Nor does the Indian nation want the means to accomplish this very modest goal—particularly in view of the vow of poverty (i.e., a minimum standard of living) that is inherent in the prosecution of Sanskrit study. But it is very much to be feared that India, in trying to Westernize suddenly, may accomplish little more than the destruction of those very cultural forms and habits of thought that have made its continued existence possible. I would consider, even today, that the potential of Sanskrit as an amalgam to the unbelievable disparity of India is unparalleled, and may in time be recognized as such.

NOTES

1. Others such as Madras Sanskrit College; Baroda Sanskrit College; the Sanskrit University, Benares; Trivandrum Sanskrit College; and the Sanskrit College within Benares Hindu University. The immediate locus of these remarks is Mahārāja's Sanskrit College (MSC), Mysore, where the writer spent one year in residence (1967–68). Though much in this paper concerns only Mysore, its typicality permits some pan-Indian generalizations on the conditions of Sanskrit education, which are freely made.

2. Such as, e.g., in Mysore State the four Sanskrit colleges attached to the *maṭhas* of the four important sects: that at Melukoṭe belonging to the Śrīvaiṣṇavas; at Uḍupi, to the Mādhvas; at Śṛṅgagiri (Śringeri) to the Smārtas; and at Siddhagaṅgā, to the Vīraśaivas.

3. One of four monasteries reputedly founded by Ādiśaṅkara himself.

4. Board for Religious and Charitable Endowments—established by the former royal government to oversee the many traditional benefactions (tax-free grants, remission of taxes, direct grants-in-aid, etc.) accorded by the ruler to legitimate cultural and scholarly undertakings. Its functions have in part been taken over by the state government.

5. The date of foundation was given to me as 1854 by the principal. I can find no confirmation of it in gazetteers or histories of Mysore. It is a continuing source of amazement to me how little attention is paid, in official documents, to the traditional institutions of education, as compared with the modern, or British-modelled ones. In this case, it seems unlikely that the Melukoṭe College has a history as old as that of the first company-sponsored college, founded by Jonathan Duncan in Benares in 1792.

6. Occasionally one meets a remarkable exception even to this rule: I was myself introduced to a gentleman—neither Brahman nor Lingāyat, but a member of the cultivator caste—who had been so attracted to the study of Sanskrit in the late thirties that he braved not only the opprobrium of the Brahmans but the strictures of his own caste to enroll in Bangalore Sanskrit College—the other royally established Sanskrit school in the old Mysore principality, which in response to many demands, was declared "public" long before Independence—in 1924 (cf. *Mysore Gazetteer*, new ed., 4:598–600). My informant went on to win a first-class traditional degree (*vidvān*)—seated on the special bench that was provided for him alone—and is now a Reader in a Western-style college. He speaks Sanskrit well—an ornament not many Brahmans can lay effective claim to. But such cases are so rare as to be a poor guide to public policy.

7. Cf. statistics supplied by Wm. Adam, ca. 1838, in his "Reports on the State of Education in Bengal," ed. S. Basu, 2d ed. (Calcutta: University of Calcutta, 1941), pp. 273, and 253–72, passim.

8. Apart, that is, from the many unorthodox Brahmans who have taken advantage of the relaxation in standards—and who probably constitute a majority of the college population today.

9. *Mysore Gazetteer*, 4:598–600.

10. The reception accorded to me, a *mleccha*, at no time by the remotest interpretation or signs suggested any other attitude than amazement and pleasure that Sanskrit—real Sanskrit and not B.A./M.A. Sanskrit—was undertaken seriously by one from across the seas. Admittedly other factors are involved—my identifiable non-Indianness (non-casteness), the rarity in these days of *any* sign of external support for the tradition, the lessening of public respect for orthodoxy and the parallel decline in the self-esteem of the orthodox; still my experience suggests that there *is*, and probably always has been, a bar that can be crossed by anyone who cultivates Sanskrit as a true medium of expression. It shows, among other things, that he has understood that Sanskrit is not so much a language, as a culture, with both a past and a future promise that few others in this world can equal.

11. A glorious example, of course, is the royal family of Mysore, whose present representative, H. H. Jayachamarajendra Wodeyar, is a distinguished Sanskritist and scholar.

12. At the high-school level, English may be taken optionally—as a substitute for *purāṇa*! Some Western-type histories of Sanskrit literature are also read at the college level.

13. Sequel to the *Report* of the Sanskrit Commission, 1956–57 (Delhi: Government of India Press, 1958), hereafter cited as *RSC*.

14. The "Up to Date List of Samskrita and Veda Patasalas, Recognized by the Department" (cyclostyled state document, dated 9th May 1968) lists 254 such schools for the entire state, 40 in Bangalore city alone!

15. The concert of lamentations has been most recently, and eloquently catalogued in the *RSC* (supra, note 13).

16. The Centre has yet to act on what appear to be the crucial recommendations: *RSC*, p. 250 (1), concerning the language formula; p. 252 (10), and pp. 253–54, concerning parity between the two educational systems.

17. *RSC*, p. 185.

18. Ibid., p. 252 (2).

19. Conforming again to a recommendation of the commission (ibid; p. 251 [9]).

20. Ibid., p. 249.

21. Ibid., pp. 249–50.

22. I was told by the registrar, Sanskrit University, Benares, that one graduate, holding the Ph.D.-equivalent degree *vacaspati*, had been admitted recently to the Indian Administrative Services examination (1968). It was hoped that the formal restriction would soon be done away with. The *RSC* is silent on these matters, but cf. p. 252, par. 6.

23. A consequence of the Mudialiar Committee *Report* (Delhi: Ministry of Education, Public Services [Qualification of Recruitment] Committee, 1955). Effects discussed in general, V. A. Pai Panandiker, *Personnel System for Development Administration* (Bombay, 1966, pp. 108–9). This restriction to *University* graduates has anticipatory analogues in earlier Indian Civil Service (I.C.S.) decisions: the Islington Commission in 1922 recommended a university degree in arts or pure sciences as an essential qualification of European officers (M. A. Muttalib, *Union Public Service Commission*, I.A.P.A., New Delhi, p. 100), and in 1939 Indians taking the I.C.S. competitive examination *in England* were "required to possess an Honours Degree of an approved British university or to have passed an equivalent examination of an approved institution of university rank. . . ." (G. P. Srivastava, *The Indian Civil Service* [New Delhi, 1965]). These reforms of course have as their main purpose upgrading performance in the higher civil-service ranks, and appear to have been considered and discussed only in those terms. I can find no reference anywhere to the dispiriting side effect these otherwise laudable initiatives have had on Sanskrit education.

24. *RSC*, pp. 253–54.

Language, Linguistics, and Politics in Tamilnad

Harold Schiffman

श्री It is probably not an exaggeration to say that of all the areas that make up the Indian Union, the state of Tamilnad (tamir̤nāḍu) has generated the most political activity over the language issue.[1] Many articles and books[2] have been written about the politics of the language issue in Tamilnad, but little has been said about the nonpolitical reasons for this development. I shall concentrate here on some of the linguistic reasons that underlie the political tension, and outline various historical linguistic processes that show quite clearly that Tamil is the modern Dravidian literary language least influenced by Indo-Aryan, a fact highly valued by Tamil speakers and one that underlies much of their resistance to the use of Hindi as a national language.

The language issue, of course, arises from the policy of the central government to implement the use of Hindi as the "official language" of the Indian Union and to curtail the use of English as the (or an) official language. To an outsider, such a policy seems quite natural, since Hindi is spoken by a "majority" of the citizenry of India, and English is the language of the colonial power, spoken only by a tiny fraction of the population. That Tamil speakers should find cause to riot, and to continue to stage demonstrations that escalate into riots for the sake of English, is incomprehensible to many. Certainly Tamil speakers do not cherish English so much that they will risk death in defense of its use. Speakers of other Dravidian languages seem to be able to learn Hindi with little or no difficulty and/or emotional distress; why then does the Tamil speaker take to the barricades over the issue of English? It seems that the comparative difficulty of Hindi versus English is not the real issue.

Most linguists would agree with the contention that, from a purely objective point of view, it is "less difficult" for a Tamilian to learn Hindi than to learn English. For example, if identical twins, native speakers of Tamil, were educated monolingually in Tamil, and one were provided with an English teacher and the other with a Hindi teacher who were equal in competence both in Tamil and in the two respective languages, and if time spent studying, methodology used, motivation of the learners, extracurricular active and passive contact (such as in movies), and so on, were equal, the twin learning Hindi would know "more" Hindi and speak it "better" than the twin learning English. That is, his Hindi would be accepted as native or near-native by a speaker of Hindi at an earlier point than the English of his twin would be accepted by a native speaker of English.

Since these ideal conditions are impossible to meet, there is a question if the hypothesis just outlined may be readily discounted as a reason for nonacceptance of Hindi. The answer is not simple; but I think our point of departure must be that the nonacceptance of Hindi has nothing to do with ease of learning, but primarily with intangibles, such as Tamil ethnic pride and language loyalty. Only secondarily does it stem from the relative availability of English teachers in Tamilnad, which is a result of the historical accident that the British gained an important hold over the subcontinent in Madras first, and thence gradually extended their power over much of South India. Since the British were in Tamilnad (then Madras) longer than anywhere else (except perhaps Bengal), English is better known in South India. Here again, this must be qualified: Indians think that English is better known in South India than elsewhere, but perhaps the truth is that the difference between the south and elsewhere is that more people in the south have a smattering of English. Whatever "better English" may mean (it would require some sort of testing program by competent linguists who supposedly have a proven method to test language proficiency to tell us whether English is "better known" or more "widespread" in the south than elsewhere), it is not important that it be a *fact* that southerners know "better English," it is only important that they *think* they know better English, for this factor to be an important one. Throughout this whole discussion, I submit that all of the factors that add up to "more nonacceptance of Hindi in Tamilnad than elsewhere in India" may or may not have any basis in *fact.* Their basis is rather in a value system that has historical roots in South Asia, and that has become deeply involved with one part of Tamilnad culture, language.

The study of the language issue in Tamilnad should begin in approximately 1000 B.C., or even earlier, for one of the cornerstones of this problem is the argument of the antiquity of Tamil culture. Tamilians know, and they are constantly being supplied with new evidence to support it, that the Dravidians antedated the Indo-Aryans on the Indian subcontinent. The Dravidian languages have not been proven to be related to any other family, and they are spread across India in a configuration that suggests that speakers of Dravidian once occupied a much larger area.[3] The isolation of the Brahui in the northwest, the coterritoriality of many of the central Dravidian languages with non-Dravidian and with Munda languages, with the contiguous languages in the south of India having the largest numbers and the oldest literary traditions, all suggest that Dravidians once occupied the whole of the subcontinent, but that their culture was "destroyed" in the north by the coming of the Aryans. The Aryans then intermarried with Dravidians or somehow imposed their language on them, not without, however, the infiltration of the Dravidian substratum into Sanskrit through the conditioning of retroflex consonants, Dravidian patterns of syntax, and so on.

Not only do Tamilians know that their language has the oldest literary tradition among the Dravidian languages (dating from the early centuries of the Christian era by the most conservative estimates), but Tamilians know that the oldest of the Tamil literature of the "Sangam" period is also the most prestigious of all Tamil literature. I think things might be different if not the oldest of the Tamil literature, but, say, the literature of the tenth century A.D. happened to be the "best" of Tamil literature. That the oldest literature is the most original suggests to Tamilians that there was an even older literature, documents from which are no longer available: upon the fact of an ancient culture, Tamilians are wont to build an elaborate myth, some of whose aspects might someday be provable, but others of which are nothing but flights of the imagination. One of the first jumps that is always made is that the Indus Valley civilization, known through the excavations at Mohenjo-Daro and Harappa, was a *Tamil* civilization. It is highly probable that the Indus Valley civilization was Dravidian, but certain advocates have assumed the probability to be fact, and have already "translated" some of the seals into Old Tamil. From there they extend Tamil influence to Mesopotamia, specifically to the Sumerians. Next the Tamils are found to be trading with the Egyptians, and so on.[4] Other well-meaning philologists, on the basis of skimpy linguistic evidence (one or two lexical items) have tried to set up phonological correspondence between Sumerian and Dravidian.[5] What is important here is not *whether* such an early Dravidian civilization might have existed. Rather, that it *might* have is taken as tantamount to an assumption that it *did*, and vague hypotheses are interpreted as if proven.

Thus we have the assumptions that Dravidian culture once extended beyond the subcontinent and was represented in its highest development by ancient Tamil culture, but was attacked and destroyed by invading Indo-Aryans, so that Dravidians are now second-class citizens in their own homeland, at least compared to the descendents of the Indo-Aryans, the Hindi speakers. Since Tamil is assumed to be more ancient than Sanskrit, and Sanskrit far more ancient than Hindi, why should Hindi be honored by being enshrined as the official language? Since almost any other language—Bengali, Telugu, or Urdu, for example—has older literary traditions than Hindi, why choose Hindi?[6]

An evaluation of the claims of the Tamils to a separate, independent, more ancient culture must include the implications of the late political incorporation into India of the ancient kingdoms of Tamilnad, the Chola (Cōṛa), Ceera (Cīra), and Pāṇḍya dynasties. The Tamil kingdoms were independent of any political control from North India until the Vijayanagar period. Admittedly, Aryan influences and Aryan culture had begun to penetrate into South India much earlier, but politically, the present Tamil and Malayalam speaking areas were not united with the north until the British period.

Thus both an ancient culture and former political independence give Tamilians great pride in their language and traditions. There is a third factor, which has only recently gained some attention, but is of particular interest to linguists. It is the idea that "Tamil" has never changed. The hypothesis of immutability reflects the phenomenon of "diglossia"[7] in Tamil, where the literary language preserves archaic features of morphology and phonology, and the spoken language reflects newer developments. So different are the two dialects of Tamil that illiterates can understand only a fraction of the spoken form of the literary language; the converse is also true, although only for non-native speakers of Tamil who learn the literary language, since native speakers, by definition, learn the spoken language first as their native tongue.

The division is denied by those[8] who claim that Tamil has never changed, since they refuse to dignify the status of spoken Tamil by calling it a language. For them, "pure," unadulterated, literary Tamil is the only Tamil; the spoken language is used only by children and illiterates. Having dismissed the spoken language as nonexistent, advocates of the purity of Tamil can add another argument to their arsenal, that of the immutability of Tamil. It is difficult to refute such arguments, of course, since they are founded upon a curious notion of what constitutes a language. What is important here is that there seems to be some correlation between the purity of Tamil and the pollution-purity notion, since the same vocabulary is used to describe "clean" Tamil (*cutta tamir̤*) as is used to describe ritually pure situations. By keeping the language ritually pure and free of change (pollution), Tamil speakers find it worthy of great devotion and respect.

Part of the aversion to spoken Tamil may stem from the large number of loans it exhibits from Indo-Aryan, English, and other sources (particularly in the Brahman dialect), which is not true of the literary language. Of course, it can be shown[9] that colloquial Tamil is in some ways older than the literary language, and that the two styles have coexisted for an extremely long period. For instance, the colloquial [anji] 'five' is found in inscriptions as early as the fifth century, although it is still written <ayntu> in the literary language today. Secondly, in a generative phonology of Tamil, some spoken forms must be taken as the underlying forms of written forms; e.g. /nālu/ 'four' (colloquial) is definitely the underlying form of <nānku> 'four' (literary), because of forms like <nār-patu> 'forty' and <nān-nūru> 'four hundred,' where the morpheme 'four' cannot easily be derived from literary <nānku>.

It is interesting to note, on the subject of diglossia, that Tamil is the Indian language characterized par excellence by diglossia. No other spoken language has a written form so different from the spoken. In Bengali and Telugu, two languages once exhibiting this phenomenon to a certain degree, movements among the literati of those languages to update their written forms have succeeded partially, Bengali under the aegis of Tagore and others, and Telugu through the works of certain modern social-realism writers. Among the other Dravidian languages, Kannada exhibits a few tendencies toward conservatism, but the spoken form is derivable by a small number of deletion and assimilation rules, for example, /heṇḍati/ 'wife' → [heṇḍti] → [heṇti]; /heṅgasu/ → [heηgsu] → [heηsu] 'woman.' In Malayalam the spoken form differs only negligibly from the written.

Furthermore, Tamil seems to be more conservative phonologically than any of the other modern literary languages. The Tamil orthography, unlike other North and South Indian scripts, has no characters to represent the voiced-voiceless distinction in consonants, and except for loan words from other languages, there is no need to do so—a single stop consonant represents a voiced consonant intervocalically and after nasals, for example, *p* is pronounced [b] between vowels and after *m*, and is pronounced [p] word-initially and when doubled: /kappal/ 'ship' is phonetically [kəppəl] while /tapāl/ 'mail' is phonetically [təba:l]. Since aspiration has not been borrowed into Tamil no aspirated consonant symbols are needed. Sanskrit /bhūmi/ 'earth' is written <pūmi> and pronounced [bu:mi]. Telugu, Kannada, and Malayalam, by contrast, have borrowed aspiration in loan words from Indo-Aryan, and have characters in their orthographies to represent these phonological contrasts.

In other ways, too, Tamil has remained conservative, such as in the retention of Proto-Dravidian /r̤/<ழ> and /ṟ/<ற> which many other languages have lost, although here Malayalam, while retaining both of these, also retains a contrast lost in Tamil, such as that between dental and alveolar nasals /n/ and /ṉ/. A more complete discussion of this phonological conservatism can be found in the literature,[10] but the main conclusion we may draw is that Tamil has resisted phonological Aryanization while the other Dravidian languages have not, and this fact is well known to Tamil speakers. Preservation of ancient phonological contrasts is not the only way in which Tamil orthography remains conservative; the most characteristic features are: the failure to represent certain sound changes, such as the lowering of the high vowels /i/ and /u/ to /e/ and /o/ respectively when preceding a single consonant and the vowel /a/, as for example LT /iṭam/, 'place' ST [yɛḍõ]; the palatalization of dental and alveolar stops to /c/ after front vowels, as in LT /paṭittēn/, ST [paṭiccẽ] 'I studied,' LT /pōyiṟṟu/, ST [pōccu] 'it went,' and the aforementioned LT /ayntu/ 'five,' ST [ancu]; the deletion of many short vowels and some non-stop consonants, as in LT /koṇṭuvā/, ST [koṇṭā] 'bring!'; and some other changes in pronominal and person-number-gender endings of verbs, as in LT /avarkaḷ/, ST [avaṅka] 'they,' LT /irukkiṟārkaḷ/, ST [irukkrāṅka] '(they) are (located)' so that a sentence like LT /avarkaḷ/ paṭittu koṇṭirukkiṟārkaḷ/ 'they are studying' has the quite different spoken form [avaṅka paṭiccikkiṭṭirukkrāṅka].

Nasalization of final vowel plus nasal sequences are quite impossible to represent in Tamil orthography, since no symbol for nasalization exists in the Tamil writing system. But this is a minor phonetic problem since nasal vowels are not systematically phonemic, and can be generated by a simple late rule in the phonology.

In contrast to the attempts to reduce diglossia and update the orthographies in other languages and writing systems, no serious movement comparable to the Bengali or Telugu modernization movements has been attempted, or to my knowledge, even proposed. Some writers do use "conversational" Tamil in their novels by means of having long dialogues between quotation marks, but this practice seems not to be accepted by all writers. In the narrative portions of novels, when spoken dialogues are not being represented, only "pure" literary Tamil is used, and many writers never represent spoken Tamil in the dialogue at all, except to represent perhaps the speech of lower-caste (and presumably illiterate) characters, children, or non-Tamils. Some writers, rather than eliminate diglossia, are in fact reintroducing forms from the oldest forms of the language, such as /yān/ 'I' to replace /nān/, which has been in use for many centuries. A deliberate effort is made to keep the two varieties of the language apart, rather than allowing the written language to gradually follow the trend of the spoken language, even if at a distance of several centuries.

This kind of Tamil writing has been called "Pandit Tamil" by Shanmugam Pillai[11] (1972), since its audience is very restricted; in fact, most educated Tamil speakers find Pandit Tamil incomprehensible. College students, for example, often attend political rallies where speeches in alliterative Pandit Tamil or DMK Tamil (the Tamil of the Dravidian nationalist political party), are delivered; even though they do not understand the content of the speeches, they respect and highly value this kind of language activity because it is, as it were, a ritual purification of the language rather than the communicative process of language.

We have then, an attitude about language that is manifested in reverence for the ancient stages of the language and attempts to keep the state of the language pure from defilement from non-Tamil and nonancient sources. This devotion is so strong that occasional devotees have resorted to self-immolation by fire to demonstrate their commitment to Tamil. As this devotion is clearly present in the culture in the framework of the purity-pollution polarity, which we know to be an ancient aspect of Indian culture, it seems clear that characterizing Tamil diglossia and concomitant antipathy to Hindi in terms of the pollution-purity polarity is not amiss. We thus can explain the intensity of the emotional content of the language issue as it applies to Tamilnadu, the conservatism of Tamil when compared with all the other languages of India, the success of the purification movement to remove all foreign and extraneous lexical items from Tamil, and the apparent contradiction of support for English alongside the intense devotion to Tamil. In the theory of social change espoused by Srinivas,[12] Westernization exists alongside Sanskritization as a motive force for upward-mobile elites. Westernization is the process that sets in when upper-caste groups are pressured too strongly from below by other upward-mobile castes. Within the language context, espousal of English is the equivalent of Westernization, and as in the Westernization/Sanskritization complex, where the same persons or groups can adopt certain modes of behavior that to an outsider appear contradictory, a Tamil speaker can cultivate his English assiduously while simultaneously maintaining his devotion to "pure" Tamil.[13] If a way to substitute Hindi for English could be found in this context, the search for a national language could be perhaps made easier. Unfortunately, Hindi does not seem to fill the bill here, probably because it does not represent a Westernizing tendency.

More work needs to be done on the relation of language to the purity-pollution concept, but I find it a fruitful analogy. It is an indigenous system, and thus explains better than any outside analytic framework what attitudes toward language are at work in the Indian linguistic subconscious. Since there is evidence that the purity-pollution polarity is stronger in South India, particularly in Tamilnadu, than elsewhere in the subcontinent, it is not surprising to find this kind of language devotion more strongly developed in the Tamil-speaking area than elsewhere.

NOTES

1. Statistics are not readily available, but it is probably safe to say that more lives have been claimed in riots over language in the Tamil areas than anywhere else in India.

2. See, for instance, Robert Hardgrave, *The Dravidian Movement* (Bombay: Popular Prakashan, 1965) or Eugene Irschick, *Politics and Social Conflict in South India: The Non-Brahman Movement and Tamil Separatism* (Berkeley and Los Angeles: University of California Press, 1969).

3. See, for instance, A. L. Basham, *The Wonder That Was India* (London: Grove Press, 1954), or M. B. Emeneau, "India as a Linguistic Area," *Language* 32 (1956):3–16.

4. P. T. Srinivas Iyengar, *History of the Tamils from the Earliest Times to 600 A.D.* (Madras: Naidu and Sons, 1929).

5. A. Sadasivam, "The Dravidian Origin of Sumerian Writing," *Proceedings of the First IATR Conference, 1966* (Kuala Lumpur: University of Malaysia Department of Indian Studies, 1968).

6. It is important to note that Hindi is given the benefit of the doubt when the status of various dialects is debated. In other words, when in doubt whether someone speaks Hindi and not something else, one decides in the favor of Hindi, but in the case of another language, gives the dialect separate status. Southerners thus feel the statistics on the number of Hindi speakers to be inflated.

7. Charles A. Ferguson, "Diglossia," *Word* 15:325–40 (1959).

8. S. Subbiah, "Is Phonetic Change Universal and Inevitable?" *Proceedings of the First IATR Conference, 1966.*

9. See, for instance, Harold Schiffman, "Morphophonemics of Tamil Numerals," *Proceedings of the First IATR Conference, 1966.*

10. Harold Schiffman, "On the Ternary Contrast in Dravidian Coronal Stops," in *Dravidian Phonological Systems*, ed. H. Schiffman and Carol

Eastman (In press). Institute for Comparative and Foreign Area Studies and University of Washington Press, Seattle.

11. M. Shanmugam Pillai, "Tamil Today," *Indian Linguistics* 33 (1972):67–71.

12. M.N. Srinivas, *Social Change in Modern India* (Berkeley and Los Angeles: University of California Press, 1965).

13. See also Milton Singer, *When a Great Tradition Modernizes* (New York: Frederick Praeger, 1972), pp. 266–67.

Author's note: Subsequent to the writing of this article and prior to its publication, R. E. Asher, in a paper entitled "Dravidian Separateness: Invention or Reality?" (*South Asian Review* 6, no. 1 (Oct. 1972):33–42), covered much of the same ground and came to many of the same conclusions.

Caste Ranking: Sacred-Secular, Tails, and Dogs

Martin Orans

श्री: A wise friend of mine in the natural sciences once told me that he carried about only light philosophical baggage so that he might easily discard it in response to the empirical world. Perhaps because I was more a devotee of the "unnatural sciences," I did not then appreciate the force of his position. This essay witnesses my change of heart; in it I espouse tentatively a number of conclusions quite uncongenial to my previous philosophical viewpoint—if I may dignify my metaphysical and empirical predispositions with so weighty a label.[1] The essay consists of a critical appraisal of McKim Marriott's article "Caste Ranking and Food Transactions: A Matrix Analysis,"[2] and an effort to relate his findings to my own as expressed in "Maximizing in Jajmaniland."[3] Marriott's predilection has been to explore minutely how Indians decide which caste is higher. This has led him to discoveries that might never have been made by someone with my penchant to emphasize secular power. Naturally I like also to think that my hunches sometimes give me an edge, quite apart from any question of skill. However that may be, Marriott's work has caused me to attempt a partial synthesis in which my own understandings undergo some change.

Already borrowing from Marriott in my previous essay, which develops a model of caste relations tested against evidence from a number of village studies, I suggested that caste ranking as revealed by card sorting and other more casual devices might approximate to the ordering by "ritual interaction" as analyzed by Kolenda,[4] but I cautioned that this relationship had not yet been properly tested. Marriott's present article deals precisely with this relationship. Utilizing a matrix form of representation of both card-sort ranking and interactional data, Marriott is able to show with great clarity just how close the relationship is between the two in Kishan Garhi, the Uttar Pradesh village that he reports on. Of those ritual interactions examined, the flow of *pakkā* food (cooked in clarified butter), *kaccā* food (not cooked in clarified butter), and *jūṭhā* (the remains of food left on plates) taken together are shown to have the closest relation to card-sort rank. Marriott concludes quite reasonably that the closeness of the fit is consistent with his long-maintained contention that such transactions form the basis for judgments of caste rank. He concludes for reasons developed in earlier works and elaborated here that what he has termed "attributes" do not substantially form such a basis. This contention will be examined later.

If his conclusion regarding the primacy of ritual interaction is correct, the rank that is attributed to a caste derives most immediately from complex observations of rank-relevant transactions between castes. The participants in these transactions are assumed to act as though guided by summations of these transactions and assumptions of transitivity. Discussing his form of representation of the system, Marriott suggests that "the matrix form of representation encourages one to look upon the set of intercaste transactions in any kind of food in Kishan Garhi as a kind of tournament among the twenty-four teams (castes) that make up this village's society. . . . Old victories and defeats are continually and inevitably reenacted in sales, gifts, feasts, and payments of many kinds."[5]

If there is a kind of tournament between castes concerned with giving and taking, one is led to inquire into the determinants of victory and defeat. Here it would be easy to introduce my secular power determinants and claim that they are the dog that wags the transactional tail. Indeed Marriott says something suggestive of this viewpoint: "If food transactions form a kind of 'economy' with a rationality of its own, that economy nevertheless overlies other analogous economic matrices having more material or political content." However, "a rationality of its own" suggests that neither economic nor political power are held completely to determine the transactional tournament.

Turning to my model of caste relations for further guidance is disappointing, since only under special conditions does it explicitly predict the rank order of castes throughout a hierarchy. There are hints in the essay supporting my model construction that may be construed as implying a one-for-one correspondence between secular power and rank, for example, "The essential underlying assumption of my model is that political and economic power (secular power) 'underlie' the ritual hierarchy. I believe this is so in part because I cannot imagine any human group would 'accept' a position of hereditary inferiority in the absence of pronounced secular inferiority."[6] But "underlie" in quotes was a deliberate weasel word meant to convey only relative importance. Furthermore, I added that "Brahmans or other priestly castes may have a somewhat higher position with respect to ritual interaction than their power or wealth would indicate."[7] But I argued that "this position and even the source of their wealth, must be supported in such an event by a caste dominant with respect to political power (the classical Brahman-Kshatriya relationship)." Obviously, other castes might similarly derive their position with the support of a dominant caste or castes though I did not consider such an eventuality. More importantly, none of these remarks was explicitly meant to predict caste rank, but rather to state conditions of stability and instability of rank. Thus I argued that consonance of ritual rank and secular power was the most stable condition of rank, and the argument about Brahmans was only meant to predict that Brahmans or a priestly caste might have a higher rank than their power would imply, without much instability.

To put the matter somewhat more precisely, the directly relevant statement from the model is the following: ritual-secular rank correlation (R) is a monotonic function of political power concentration (P), holding Jajmani-market continuum (J) constant; and ritual-secular rank correlation (R) is a function of Jajmani-market continuum (J) holding political power concentration (P) constant; $R = f_3 (P, J)$. R is defined as the fit between rank of castes as indicated by card sorting or transactions with secular rank; the highest R would obtain in the event that the ritual and secular rank of each caste was the same. P is a measure of the concentration by caste of political power; the highest P would obtain in the event that a single caste monopolized political power. *J* is a measure of the degree to which the flow of valuables and associated relations between castes are held to be governed by traditional ties; a high *J* obtains in the event that such "prices" and relations resist fluctuations in supply and demand. Therefore, the model predicts caste rank only under conditions of high *P* and *J*, in which event an approximate one-to-one correspondence is implied since stability of rank throughout the hierarchy was held to be a monotonic function of *R* and *P* [$S = f_2(P, R)$]; one might also conclude that under highly stable conditions there would be a similar close correspondence of ritual and secular rank. My model, therefore, only predicts caste rank specifically under conditions of high *P* and *J* or high stability (*S*). Though the data used to test the theory support the connections between variables indicated by the model, the crude manner in which *R* was estimated do not entitle us to assume anything like a one-to-one correspondence in those cases where *R* was scored as maximum.

Though Marriott's presentation of caste in Kishan Garhi is in many respects quite detailed, there is not sufficient information to determine precisely the connection between secular power and rank. Marriott does provide numbers and land rent by caste, and though these do not closely approximate the many rank distinctions made, it is not clear how closely land rent approximates the total wealth of the various castes. It is, however, noteworthy that the highest and dominant caste, the Sanadhya Brahmans, have about three times as many families as their nearest rivals in number, the Jat cultivators, who fall in the second rank of castes; in addition, the Brahmans hold land whose rental value was over four times that of their nearest competitors, the Baghele goatherds, and this rent amounts to over half the total land rent in the village.

Marriott's evidence concerning the mobility of the Baghele goatherds indicates that if the model was correct about the independent effect of the concentration of political power (*P*) on the correlation between ritual and secular rank (*R*), it was correct for reasons that are partially incorrect. I had reasoned that concentrated political power would serve to prevent changes in both attributes: ritual interaction and economic status, thereby maintaining a high correlation between ritual and secular rank. However, where a change in secular rank (e.g., economic power) does occur, preservation of ritual interaction would not result in preserving a high correlation, but, on the contrary, would have the opposite effect. The case of the goatherds illustrates this outcome quite clearly.

During the 30s, the goatherds became one of the richest groups. Doubtlessly motivated by desire to improve their rank they undertook the following transformations of the interactions: (1) ceased accepting both *kaccā* and *pakkā* food from some castes and succeeded in giving *kaccā* food to some who had not previously received it from them; (2) richly paid waterman and barber castes "to provide their fullest services at feasts." But the Kachi cultivators (ranked just above the goatherds in the card sort and equal to them in food transactions) prevailed on some Brahmans indebted to them to help curtail the goatherd upstarts. "Brahmans then threatened to discharge barbers . . . if the barbers picked up the garbage-soiled plates at goatherd feasts."[8] In a compromise resolution, the goatherds kept their barbers ("at high rates")—while excusing them from the garbage-connected duties.[9]

The outcome of these changes seems to be that the goatherds have raised their rank (presumably a previous card sort would have placed them lower), but not as much as their transaction improvement would indicate; doubtless their wealth would entitle them to an even higher position than that presently accorded. But from a theoretical point of view, it would seem that the dominance of the Brahmans was instrumental in preventing the goatherds from achieving a rank commensurate with their wealth or at least their improved transactions; Brahmans intervened to prevent further transactional improvement, thus limiting the goatherds' mobility. Therefore, the high concentration of political power in Kishan Garhi associated with Brahman dominance seems to have prevented a closer correspondence between secular power (here wealth) and rank; in this respect concentrated political power seems to result in a lower correlation between secular power and ritual rank! Since this process seems quite plausible and no doubt general, how can it be reconciled with the direct relation between concentration of political power and the correlation between ritual and secular rank confirmed by my previous investigation? The answer would seem to be that concentrated political power more often succeeds in preventing economic change and maintaining consonance than in retarding consonance by preserving anomalous interactions.

But the central concern of this paper is still before us: what are the relations between secular power, ritual interaction, and attributes, for it is an understanding of this linkage that would join my findings with those of Marriott. As indicated earlier, Marriott holds that it is primarily ritual interaction and not attributes that actually guide judgments about caste rank.

Let us first examine why Marriott believes attributes are much less relevant than interaction in symbolizing the hierarchy. The following arguments seem most relevant:

1. If ritual purity in Hindu terms were relevant, how is it that the villagers of Kishan Garhi where Marriott first carried out field work ranked him in the third position beneath the Jats? Marriott cites his own high rank as contradictory to an attribute theory, because in certain respects his Euro-American life style runs counter to widely praised principles of high Hinduism, for example, eating habits. This is certainly a very telling argument, at least for this one instance of rank assignment. Furthermore, in a personal communication Marriott detailed how food transactions consistent with his high status gradually developed. It seems plausible from his account that having seen certain others of putatively high rank accept food from Marriott, others were persuaded to do likewise.

Granting all of this, what remains to account for the high ritual interaction that Marriott was able to establish? He would accept the relevance of secular power but deny the relevance of attributes. But if that is generally the case, then there should be a perfect correspondence between ritual interaction and secular power. However, both Marriott and I agree that this is not the case; therefore, attributes do count for something, or some other variable accounts for the discrepancies between ritual interaction and secular power. For Marriott this other variable would be observation of exogenous interactions.

I can think of at least two closely related attributes that may have contributed to Marriott's high status. The first is that he was relatively wealthy. Here I refer to his wealth per se rather than what it could command; perhaps wealth is always a relevant attribute per se. Secondly, he belongs to the *jāti* "Euro-American," which everywhere has a local designation and reputation. This is a well-known powerful and prestigeful *jāti*, however distasteful some of their habits. Thus we might infer the existence of "a list" of caste-ethnic named groups having various ranks, as my Africanist colleague David Kronenfeld has suggested. Since it is difficult to disentangle wealth per se from what it buys, let us pose a case that would test the relevance of the list attribute: What if everything had been the same but Marriott had been a "sweeper" by *jāti*; might it not have made a difference?

But what of castes that are not powerful at all; how do they enter the system and maintain or not maintain their position? My model might suggest that their various minute differences in secular power are weighed and they are then placed accordingly. This would certainly lead to a close fit between ritual interaction or card sort rank and secular power and thereby serve consensus and stability; increases in secular power might both facilitate higher forms of interaction and cause other castes to acknowledge increased power and thereby acknowledge a higher place on the list. Since they are higher, it becomes right to accept their food; since one accepts their food, they are higher. That food transactions are essential symbols of rank makes a difference, if it is so, because food is a symbol with uses beyond its symbolism. Those who can provide more of it can tempt those who have less into an exchange of food for esteem. In addition, the acceptance of *kaccā* food symbolizes not only inferior status but probably also the acceptance of a variety of similarly valuable perquisites exchanged for esteem and, perhaps, for virtue. Acceptance of the food of inferiority very well symbolizes dependence and inferior rank.

2. There is not a one-for-one correspondence between any of the attributes cited and caste rank throughout the hierarchy. This would seem to be the case, but of course, as Marriott notes, an index of attributes might yield such a correspondence. He suggests that this is somewhat implausible because of the complexity of weighting and calculation involved given the relatively high consensus that prevails. But there is another possibility, that is, that certain attributes function over only a part of the hierarchy like the very well-known one of wearing the sacred thread that is restricted in high Hinduism to those "twice born" and associated with the three highest *varṇa*. This possibility corresponds with many of the remarks of Marriott's informants, for example, living in forts and mansions, wearing the thread, being a Brahman and purifier of the world, and so on. This may all only amount to ex

post facto rationalization, but I don't yet see that this has been proved. *Furthermore, if attributes combine with secular power to produce both ritual interaction and card-sorting rank, one would not expect a one-to-one correspondence since secular power would vary independently of attributes.*

3. Some of the attributes mentioned as rank-relevant are in fact characteristic of all or many castes. These might be of some rank value, but obviously they do not differentiate in fact.

4. The pollution-purity attributes do not operate as a basic underlying ideology of caste rank because the handling of polluted materials, and so on, is only rank-relevant when performed as a service for another caste. Here Marriott presents a number of telling examples clarifying the complementary nature of pollution and purity. A solid case is made for the argument that very little, if anything, is polluting in such a way as to be of rank value except where it has been specially so designated.

5. The attributes of some castes were not regarded by others as uniformly high; nevertheless, consensus on rank is quite high.

6. Attributes of high value at one time may not be of high value at another time, that is attribute values change. Overwhelming evidence on this point makes it clear that there is certainly no steady set of attributes that hold rank constant through time. But does it follow that attributes vary randomly with rank, and can changes in attributes affect rank?

The remarks that Indians have made to Marriott and others about caste rank suggest, as many have noted, a secular power aspect of caste rank and a sacred or moral aspect of rank. Perhaps most analysts would agree with Marriott and me that secular power plays a substantial role in the operation of the system. The point of contention is perhaps what kind of a role does the sacred and moral play and how is it interwoven with the secular? At one extreme the sacred-moral might be regarded like interactional symbols as mere appendage to the secular dog; is such an extreme position justified?

A glance at caste ranking elsewhere, plus my general recollection, seems to create serious doubt about the extreme secular position. For example, if one compares Marriott's ranks with those given by Wiser for Uttar Pradesh village, one notes the following:[10] there are six castes with the same name; their names and relative order in Wiser are: Brahman, Kachi (gardener), Darzi (tailor), Bhangi (sweeper), Faqir (Muslim devotee), Manihar (Muslim bangleman).[11]

The order of Hindu castes is exactly the same in Marriott's village. There is, however, a significant reversal between Muslim and Hindu ranks, with the Bhangi sweeper below the Muslims in Marriott's village. If one compares a number of relatively menial occupations found in both villages without regard to the caste name of those performing the occupation, one obtains the following correspondence: waterman, potter, washerman, leather worker, sweeper.

There is no reversal of this ranking in Marriott. Similar results are suggested in a comparison of both these villages with Mayer's Malwa village,[12] even though it is some distance removed and part of a different local tradition. Although I have not systematically carried out such research, I believe that there are regional ranking systems with more than chance association of ranks and some tendencies with an extremely wide interregional association. If a caste always entered the system according to its secular power, if it maintained or altered its position freely with changes in secular power, I do not think the correspondence of ranks observed within a region and even between regions would be as high as it is. In terms of interactions, one might defend the Marriott position by asserting that the similarity of ranking within a region and even between regions was the result of mutual observation of interaction, but as indicated earlier, it would be difficult to account for maintenance of such similarity. Why should secular fluctuations presumably related to such factors as the supply and demand of services lead to such similar outcomes? Is it really thinkable that the petty differences in wealth characteristic of most lower castes is so minutely measured on entrance as to result in a similar rank throughout a wide region? I rather think that we have here a dog both secular and moral and that both the Brahman (priestly) rank, where it is incommensurate with secular power, and many of the ranks below the top can only be accounted for by consideration of the entire animal. Insofar as my model suggested a one-for-one correspondence between secular and ritual rank as more than a highly stable condition, I think it was in error. And though I was probably correct in suggesting that such a correspondence is increased by concentrated political power and *jajmāni* relations (with the modifications suggested earlier), I now think a certain discrepancy between secular and sacred rank may be a common occurrence. Such a discrepancy like the Kṣatriya acceptance of Brahman ritual superiority results in casting a moral aura on the entire system. Whether or not this is actually perceived by those at the top, it seems that there is a moral-secular trade off in the ranking game.

Those who come into the system without much power are ranked heavily on the basis of a moral ideology. Their caste name may have a place on a list. Associated with the place on the list are various attributes, that is, morally valued or disvalued characteristics; naturally these are commensurate with the place on the list, although such attributes may be selectively invoked to justify a place on the list retrospectively. Thus, for example, a sweeper is on the bottom of the list in many parts of South Asia, and I do not imagine that an Indian, when asked to place a sweeper, thinks about food exchange *and then* concludes that sweepers are low. No doubt such interaction reflects this low status and even reinforces the perception, but I do not think that it is psychologically prior. Supposing it were the case that Indians from a particular village had a notion that a particular caste had a certain position on the list and they were to observe that others interacted with this caste in a manner incommensurate with their estimate. No doubt this inconsistency might cause them to reflect upon the place they had accorded the caste and perhaps might even cause them to alter this position. Thus Marriott would be correct in his estimate that observation of inconsistent interaction might affect consensus, and that such observation may be important in establishing the position of a caste in a region. Similarly, I imagine that if one hears that others place a caste differently on their list, one might be induced to reconsider his own list and interactions.

Supposing that a caste has just enough resources to induce some castes higher on the list to accept an altered set of food transactions consistent with a reversal in rank; or put differently, suppose a caste is asked to exchange rank for wealth as in the case of the Baghele goatherds; those higher up, however, may have some interest in maintaining a stable list, commensurate attributes and commensurate transactions. Their interference might then prevent both transactional change and change in the list. The Baghele case seems to be one in which such trade offs took place; they had sufficient wealth to induce a greater improvement in rank than they have so far attained, but the influence of the Brahmans atop the system curtailed their gain. They got some improvement in their place on the list, but not even quite what their transactional position would now warrant. They also got some of the transactional improvement that they desired, but because of the Brahmans, not all that their wealth might obtain. Presumably, every caste accepts, in some degree, a set of attributes as complexly related to its list. While it does not follow that these will be invoked by themselves to determine place on the list and interactions, each caste will require some inducement to alter such judgments. Very powerful castes will more easily induce others to regard their attributes as high, however inconsistent with what is thought valuable. This no doubt partly accounts for the kind of temporal fluctuations in attribute evaluation noted by Marriott. Powerful castes always have high attributes, since either those less powerful will change their evaluation or the powerful caste will change its attributes, cashing them in for moral rectitude. Though there is abundant historical evidence of this process, there is also evidence of shifts in moral sensibility that are partially independent of local power situations, for example, vegetarianism, teetotalism, and so on. Such shifts may result in inconsistencies between attributes and rank.

If there are such complex trade offs, it would follow that such processes as "Sanskritization" or emulation of prevailing high moral practices, that is, those associated with a high position on the list, ought to facilitate rank improvement. It would also follow that it would take less of an increase in secular power to improve one's place on the list if one adopts or has the right attributes.

There is no doubt that attribute inconsistency creates dissonance, but such dissonance may be dealt with in several ways. We know that traditionally various key attributes of rank value, such as reading and reciting the Vedas, wearing the sacred thread, and so on, were forbidden to lower castes. Often the reaction to attribute rank inconsistency has been to despise the emulators on the grounds that they are striving beyond their station. Both our theoretical understanding and the empirical evidence show that there have been very few, if any, instances of rank improvement resulting exclusively from improvements in attributes. But avoiding dissonance should have some value reflected, perhaps in the price of rank attainment. If one has the attribute of being, for example, a Brahman, that is, some relevant set of rankers accept the claim, he is likely to enter a hierarchy at or near the top (in a Hindu region) regardless of his wealth or political power. Indeed, he is likely to acquire some of both by virtue of being a Brahman. Even if some Brahmans happen to fall in secular power they are likely to retain their rank for some time; however, over a long period under such adverse conditions, people may cease to accept the hereditary claim, thereby restoring correlation between secular power and ritual interaction. The same argument in reverse would apply to low castes like Chamars (leatherworkers). For them to enter a system as a high caste, they would have to either possess so much power (like Euro-Americans) as to bring about a partial reappraisal of attributes or claim to be really of high caste, for example, Rajputs. But if it were known they were Chamars, they would require more power than Brahmans to attain equal rank. Thus castes with high attributes will enter a system higher than those of low attributes with equal power, will maintain their positions with less power, and can attain higher status with less power.

We are now in a position to summarize tentative conclusions and point to unanswered questions.

1. There is a close correspondence between ritual interactions and rank as expressed in card sorting. Perhaps this is generally true.

2. The correspondence between ritual interaction and rank throughout the hierarchy appears to be closer than the correspondence between any particular attribute and rank. Perhaps this is generally true.

3. The case of the Baghele goatherds is one in which a discrepant increase in secular power is consistent with an increase in ritual interaction and rank.

4. The increase in rank of the goatherds is less than the increase in ritual interaction would indicate. Previous lower ritual interaction may be the explanation, as Marriott suggests, and/or previous or present lower attributes.

5. The political-economic power of the dominant Brahmans seems to have been critical in preventing the Baghele goatherds from obtaining all the improvement in ritual interaction that their

wealth might command. Therefore, concentrated secular power may inhibit a close correspondence between ritual interaction and/or rank with economic power. To reconcile this with my previous finding, that concentrated political power contributes directly to the correlation between secular power and ritual rank, I suggest that concentrated political power is more effective in preventing economic change than ineffective by retarding commensurate change in ritual interaction.

6. Under conditions of highly concentrated secular power, there will not be such a close connection throughout the hierarchy between the secular power of each caste and its rank as my model suggested. Such discrepancy may arise as suggested in number 5, above, that is, a caste that improves its secular power may be prevented from improving its ritual interaction and/or its rank; concentrated power and attributes or previous ritual interaction may combine to produce this result. Similarly, castes whose secular power declines may be able, up to a point, to maintain their ritual interaction, attributes, and rank, but the use of food transactions as ritual interaction makes this symbol particularly vulnerable to decline in economic power. Thus a fall in economic power rather than a rise would more likely lead to a nearly commensurate rank. Therefore, the form of the tournament has some significance of its own, as Marriott suggests. Discrepancies may also arise through entrance into the system of castes with high attributes but less secular power. All of these discrepancies depend, however, on the support of a dominant caste or castes with a vested interest in maintaining the moral integrity of the system.

7. The significance of some attributes is suggested by the similarity of rank of a number of castes within a region and even between regions; it does not seem that secular power alone would produce such an outcome. Marriott would, however, probably attribute such discrepancy to observation of exogenous ritual interaction.

8. The suggested significance of attributes combined with the criticisms of attributes provided by Marriott leads me to suggest the following:

a. there may be a list attribute that Marriott has not considered, that is, the names of certain castes may immediately suggest a rank;

b. some attributes associated with the list, like polluting or ennobling occupations, may be significant at some points of the hierarchy;

c. it is possible that secular power and (other?) attributes may combine to influence rank;

d. discrepant secular power has resulted in certain instances in change of ritual interaction and/or attributes; some of these changes have been followed by a change in rank, but we do not know if either was necessary to the ensuing change in rank;

e. extremely dominant castes or other social entities can bring about a change in the evaluation of attributes; in this event at least, a change in attributes is not a necessary condition for a change in rank;

f. a discrepancy between secular power and rank may be a necessary condition to a change in rank;

g. since caste rank is pervaded by an ideology of hereditary status, former attributes and former ritual interaction, as Marriott suggests, may limit the significance of changes of either in effecting rank alteration. Therefore, old attributes might make a difference, but for a while new ones might not;

h. change in secular power may be a necessary condition for change of rank; one can see how improvement in food transactions would contribute to such a condition;

i. if, in complex interaction, secular power and attributes affect rank and/or ritual interaction, neither might be in as close correspondence with rank as is ritual interaction.

Obviously no synchronic analysis relating ritual interaction and card-sort rank can determine whether or not attributes (including the list attribute) affect ritual interaction, and thereby affect card-sort rank, since even if ritual interaction were in perfect correspondence with card-sort rank the dynamic effects would not be ruled out. In a preliminary effort to solve the static question of what dimensions are directly taken into account by one ranking castes, Kathleen Smith has ingeniously applied the techniques of "multidimensional scaling" to the problem.[13] Using Marriott's card-sort data, the card-sort data provided by Freed,[14] and ritual-interaction data provided by Freed, she finds that all three sets of data are best represented in three (not one) dimension![15] This finding would tend to support my static interpretation rather than Marriott's. However, the technique employed produces results that are suggestive rather than definitive, and capable of innumerable interpretations other than multi-causality in the sense that I intend. To settle the static question and resolve the interpretation of Smith's finding, one would have to fill in the appropriate power and attribute data and match it with the dimensions that appear in her findings. No one has yet provided all the data necessary for such analysis.

To disentangle the complex connections between the variables that determine card-sort rank we shall have to employ multiple regression analysis, or at least partial and multiple correlations on appropriate data; we shall have to apply such analysis with a clear eye on a causal model or we shall simply discover repeatedly what we already know with some reliability, that is, all the variables we have been concerned with are highly intercorrelated.

Marriott's investigation of the interactions symbolic of caste rank has led me to a greater appreciation of the importance of the symbols themselves. But his findings also suggest a greater significance of certain attributes than either he or I have claimed. In attempting to join his understandings and my own I have found it necessary to make more explicit my own causal model of caste ranking and to compare it with what I take to be Marriott's model. Though the differences that remain are not great, I would hope that my attempt to formalize both models will stimulate relevant empirical inquiry. That would indeed justify my labor.

To facilitate empirical inquiries aimed at deciding between Marriott's view and my own (modified often by Marriott's), the following diagrammatic representation of hypothetical causal processes is offered:

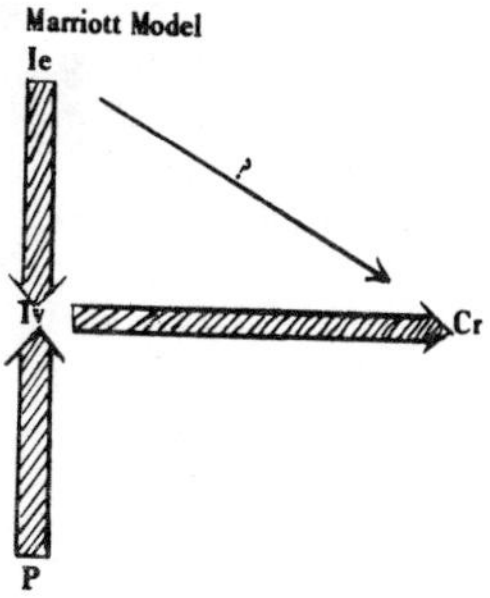

Symbols

Cr=Card-sort rank (by an individual or by the village) of a caste

Iv=Ritual interaction in the village pertinent to the caste being ranked

Ie=Ritual interaction observed elsewhere

P =Power, economic and political of the caste being ranked

Arrows indicate direction of causality; their thickness, strength of determination

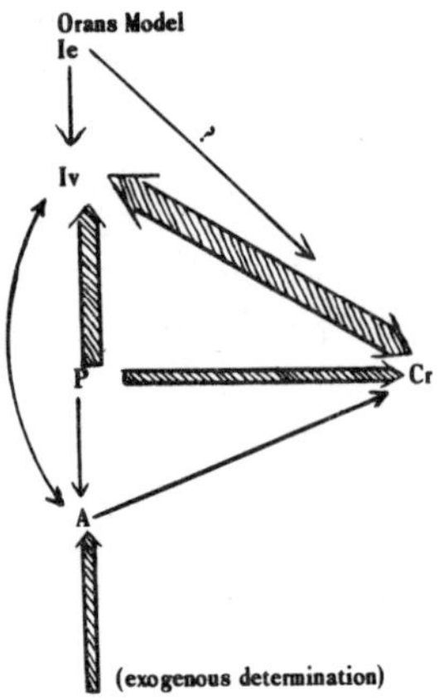

Symbols same as above with addition of:
A = Attributes
(in addition Cr is taken to be reflective of the "list attribute" and therefore is itself depicted as a causal agent

NOTES

1. This essay emerged from discussions with my colleague in history, Burton Stein of the University of Hawaii.

2. In *Structure and Change in Indian Society*, ed. Milton Singer and Bernard S. Cohn (Chicago: Aldine Publishing Company, 1968).

3. *American Anthropologist* 70, no. 5 (1968).

4. Pauline Mahar Kolenda, "A Multiple Scaling Technique for Caste Ranking," *Man in India* 39 (1959):127–47.

5. Marriott, "Caste Ranking and Food Transactions," p. 155.

6. Orans, "Maximizing in Jajmaniland," p. 878.

7. Ibid., p. 880.

8. Marriott, "Caste Ranking and Food Transactions," p. 164.

9. Ibid.

10. William H. Wiser, *Hindu Jajmani System* (Lucknow: Lucknow Publishing House, 1936).

11. Ibid., pp. 7–8.

12. Adrian C. Mayer, *Caste and Kinship in Central India: A Village and Its Region* (Berkeley and Los Angeles: University of California Press, 1960).

13. Kathleen Smith, "The Multidimensional Nature of Indian Caste Ranking and Ritual Exchange."

14. Stanley A. Freed, "An Objective Method for Determining the Collective Cost Hierarchy of an Indian Village," *American Anthropologist* 65 (1963):879–81; "Caste Ranking and the Exchange of Food and Water in a North Indian Village," *Anthropological Quarterly* 43, pt. 2, no. 1 (1963): 1–14.

The Multileveled Ontology of Advaita Vedānta

Eliot Deutsch

श्रीः Advaita Vedānta, the nondualistic school of Indian philosophy expounded by Śaṃkara in the eighth and ninth centuries, advocates a *Weltanschauung* that is based on the belief that the world is constituted by incommensurable levels of being. The levels are (1) absolute being (*pāramārthika*)—the undifferentiated, qualityless, oneness, or fullness of being; (2) practical or empirical being (*vyāvahārika*)—the differentiated, multiple world of our ordinary experience, and (3) illusory being (*prātibhāsika*—objects related to experiences of hallucination, pure fancy, erroneous sense-perception and the like. According to Śaṃkara, the first level of being, the Absolute or Brahman, is alone fully real and, when once experienced, negates the other two levels—that is, relegates them to a kind of unreality.

Nevertheless, until such time as the Absolute is realized directly in one's own experience, one is called upon to acknowledge the existence of the three levels: absolute being, practical being, and illusory being. These levels, the Advaitin claims, are actual contents of experience. Practical being and illusory being are not completely unreal or nonbeing (*tuccha*; *asat*), like the son of a barren woman (to use the stock Advaitin example) or a square circle, precisely because they are experienceable. The completely unreal can never, according to the Advaitin, be a content of experience.

The purpose of this paper is to examine some of the epistemological and axiological implications of this multileveled ontology (implications that are explicitly made and accepted by Advaita Vedānta) and to offer a general philosophical appraisal of it.

Before we can examine the implications of the ontology, though, we need first to look at the manner in which Advaita sets forth and justifies its levels of being. It does this on what it takes to be the results of spiritual experience and on what it sees to be the requirements or dictates of reason.

From the standpoint of experience, the advaitin holds that man has the capacity for an extremely varied experience and that some of his experiences are fundamentally different in kind from others. There is, he affirms, a form of experience that discloses the fundamental identity between the self (*ātman*) and reality (*brahman*). This experience, sometimes called *nirvikalpa samādhi*, is an intuitive, immediate insight into the ground of one's being. It is celebrated by the Advaitin as an experience of perfect insight, of fully awakened consciousness, of total bliss (*ānanda*). The experience of oneness, he maintains, is so complete and overpowering that it renders all other experience as insignificant. The experience of reality is thus not comparable to any other human experience. It is *sui generis*; it is ineffable, unique, and self-certifying.

But the greatest part of our experience is clearly not nondual in character. It is constituted rather by basic subject/object distinctions, by multiple forms, by linguistic designations, by spatio-temporal determinations, by complex judgments and valuations. Our ordinary experience is subject to constant change, to contradictions, to the fits and starts, ups and downs, of emotion and passion. Our experience in this practical, relative, or empirical world is contextual and nonenduring.

Closely associated with this world of our ordinary experience that constitutes the empirical or practical level of being is the illusory experience (which occupies, for purpose of analogy, a very important place in Advaitic thought). This type of experience is commonplace. Everyone, at one time or another has experienced an illusion. An experience has the character of an illusion when it is contradicted by objective and repeatable experience and when it lacks practical character. The mirage in the desert cannot quench one's thirst. The illusion disappears when a further knowledge of the conditions under which the illusion is present is gained.

For most persons the last two domains, the empirical and the illusory, are taken as inclusive of life. The Advaitin himself, as we have seen, insists that the world associated with this experience is necessarily taken as real and adequate by one who lacks the experience of oneness. Sureśvara, an important follower of Śaṃkara, states simply and directly that "there is no reason to call the world unreal *before* the knowledge of the oneness of the Self (has been attained)."[1]

But it is possible, according to Śaṃkara, to at least show to such a person the possibility, and indeed rational necessity, for the first, primal level of being. From the standpoint of reason, the Advaitin argues that the moment one accepts the distinction between practical being and illusory being one is driven to accept the further distinction between both of these levels of being and reality. He argues thus: If there were no reality or absolute being, neither practical being nor illusory being would be possible, for whatever we take to be real at the level of phenomenal experience always has a ground or locus (*adhiṣṭhāna*) for its reality. Appealing to the example of someone who believes that a piece of rope is a snake (and acts accordingly) and then later discovers that it is indeed but a piece of rope, Śaṃkara writes:

> Whenever we deny something unreal, we do so with reference to something real: the unreal snake, e.g., is negatived with reference to the real rope. But this (denial of something unreal with reference to something real) is possible only if some entity is left. If everything is denied, no entity is left, and if no entity is left, the denial of some other entity which we may wish to undertake, becomes impossible, i.e., that latter entity becomes real and as such cannot be negatived."[2]

An illusion, in short, is correctable only by reference to something real. We learn that the object that we took to be a snake is not a snake only when we learn that it is in fact a piece of rope. The world, if it is to have any kind of reality, if it is to be the content of experience, must have its ground in a more encompassing, permanent state of being. The world of our ordinary experience can be contradicted, just as the imagined snake in the rope, and hence rationally one must affirm an absolute reality (*pāramārthika*; Brahman or Ātman) as the necessary ground of being. I leave it to you to judge the rightness or validity of this argument.

Let us examine now the implications of this multileveled ontology. First of all, epistemologically it follows from the positing of reality as incommensurable with the world of our ordinary experience that it is impossible for us to know reality in the terms or by the categories of intellectual understanding. Reason functions only where there are distinctions, where there are names and forms (*nāma-rūpa*), where there are spatio-temporal determinations. In the *Kena Upaniṣad* we read:

> It [Absolute being; Reality] is conceived of
> by him by whom it is not conceived of.
> He by whom It is conceived of, knows It not.
> It is not understood by those who (say they)
> understand It.
> It is understood by those who (say they) understand It not.[3]

Real knowledge, then, as contrasted to the pretensions of abstract, formal knowledge (which knows by observation, separations, divisions, categories, concepts) is a kind of recognition—an immediate insight that transcends all subject/object distinctions. It is a matter of *realization* rather than *learning*. Insight as such cannot be taught; it can only be directly achieved. Rational proof or logical demonstration (mental activities that can be taught) cannot bring one to a realization of reality; they do not have the capacity to know or to explain reality.

And it also follows that it is impossible for us ever to explain fully or adequately the world of our ordinary experience. If the levels of being are incommensurable, then we cannot reason from one to the other. We can never, in other words, account causally for the origin of our world by referring it to absolute being. We might be able to see how empirical being is necessarily grounded in absolute being, but we cannot explain one in terms of the other. Also, we cannot explain with absolute certainty the structure or course of any phenomenon in nature. Relativity of judgment is the rule of the empirical. Experience changes and the mind that would explain this change with certainty is part and parcel of the change. All knowledge and explanation of our ordinary experience is thus touched with a kind of ignorance (*avidyā*). It is necessarily a partial or lower knowledge (*aparā vidyā*) as contrasted with the intuitive or higher knowledge of reality (*parā vidyā*). The world cannot be characterized, then, according as these terms are defined by Vedānta, as either real or unreal (*sadasadvilakṣaṇa*). The world, in essence, is unknowable. It is inexpressible (*anirvacanīya*). It is *māyā*—a creative illusion that resists all final or complete explanation.

We can, nevertheless, according to Advaita, achieve a partial and pragmatically effective knowledge of our world and this knowledge, the Advaitin concludes, does hold good when it is accepted in its own terms—that is, as partial and relative. Each way of knowing has its appropriate criterion of validity. Sense-perception, inference, all the so-called *pramāṇas* or means of valid knowledge can achieve a rightness appropriate to themselves. Reason is justified in its proper operation of drawing out the relations that obtain between objects of sense experience and of establishing, analogically, the basic principles of metaphysics. Reason, in other words, does have its proper place and its appropriate canons of truth and validity. It is confined to the world of sense experience, but this confinement does not mean that it has no proper function to perform.

To those of us accustomed to either/or, yes or no, ways of thinking this denial of reason on the one hand and affirmation of it on the other seem very strange. It is, though, a natural conclusion or implication of a multileveled ontology. What is true or adequate at one level is not necessarily (and indeed seldom is) true or adequate on another level. But because of the incommensurable nature of the levels one level does not disturb another in its own internal affairs. A higher level of being, by its nature, makes another level qualitatively lower and precludes any claim on the lower level to ultimacy. But that is all that it does.

Another epistemological implication of the multileveled ontology of Advaita Vedānta, and one that should be of some interest to both devotees and detractors of Indian thought, is that an understanding of the real (a realization of reality) does not give one any special or privileged knowledge of phenomenal experience

—that is, of particulars, of individual objects and their relations in past, present, or future time. According to the manner in which absolute being is affirmed by the Advaitin, the empirical world disappears from consciousness upon the attainment of the oneness of being. Reality cannot speak the language of multiplicity. "Knowledge and ignorance," Śaṃkara writes, "cannot co-exist in the same individual, for they are contradictory like light and darkness."[4] *Parā vidyā*, the higher knowledge of reality, is not, then, a supernatural, magical knowledge of the world. The higher knowledge, Śaṃkara states, "only removes the false notion [about the world's alleged independent reality], it does not create anything [new]."[5] Just as the knowledge that the supposed snake is only a rope does not tell one anything about snakes, so an insight into reality does not reveal any facts about the world beyond the fact of its relative empirical status. For Advaita Vedānta, there can be no magical, Faustian knowledge that is acquired or that is acquirable from the realization of oneness.

This leads us to some axiological or value implications of Advaita's multileveled ontology. The first and obvious implication is that an insight into reality is entirely in the domain of value. Knowledge of reality, or self-knowledge, according to Advaita, is a "saving" knowledge: it provides a complete liberation (*mokṣa*) from the bondage of the world. Reality is a state of freedom; negatively, it is a freedom from the chains of *karma*, of conditioned action; positively, it is a freedom for peace and blessedness. Freedom means self-realization; the power to determine oneself, the power to have one's action be a reflection of one's deepest nature; and this freedom is the very content of the experience of reality. For Advaita Vedānta, reality is value and the highest value for man is its realization.

On the level of our ordinary experience (*vyāvahārika*), it follows that the major, if not sole, criterion that is appropriate for the judgment of acts and intentions is: that act or intention that promotes the attainment of the highest value is "good," that which hinders the attainment is "bad." Man's true *dharma* or law of his nature is for him to attain self-knowledge, to realize reality. While accepting the basic pattern of social structure, of duties and responsibilities, for one who is working in the world (as a student, householder, etc.), the Advaitin claims that this must be transcended. Good deeds and obligatory acts, as defined by conventional morality, cannot by themselves produce the realization of reality. Morality might be an aid to this realization, but it is neither a necessary nor sufficient condition for it. Knowledge alone, according to Advaita, is the source of enlightenment.

This leads to a very interesting and, for many Westerners, disturbing conclusion: the end does justify the means provided that the end is spiritual enlightenment.

For the Advaitin, as for many other Indian thinkers, it is entirely proper for one to employ various devices or subterfuges in one's effort to help another person attain *mokṣa.* The end need not be commensurate with the means, for once again they occupy different and incommensurable levels of being. This implication is brought out very vividly in much of the literature of Indian philosophy that deals with teacher/student (or better) *guru*/disciple relationships. The *Bhagavad Gītā,* for example, constantly employs the device of leading Arjuna, the disciple to higher levels of understanding by appealing to the demands of his present state of being, often to the forms of his own troubled ego. Arjuna is told by Kṛṣṇa, the divine *guru,* that he must fight in a just war because if he doesn't his enemies will call him a coward, or because he has only to gain by doing so. In this context, fighting in the just war means for Arjuna the carrying out and fulfillment of his *dharma* as a *kṣatriya,* a fulfillment that is a necessary condition for his spiritual advancement. In Buddhism, also, we find many examples of this implication. In the *Saddharma Puṇḍarīka* there is the famous parable of the burning house, which tells about how a man comes home to find his house on fire and his children, unaware of it, playing games inside. He calls to them but they pay him no heed. He then entices them outside by promising them all sorts of wonderful things and then they hear him and respond. Each person can respond to a teaching only on the level of his own developed understanding. Even if it involves what we might call "intellectual dishonesty," the means employed to help another attain *mokṣa* are justified by that end which is the highest value.

With the affirmation of a highest value that is incommensurable with empirical being, it also follows that none of the values or moral judgments that we make can legitimately be taken by us as final or complete. Reality is "beyond good and evil"; all value judgments are made from the standpoint of *avidyā*, from the standpoint of our involvement in the world. They may be justified pragmatically and even rationally in terms of the necessities of social relationship, but again they must be transcended for reality to shine in consciousness. Value judgments, like all ordinary knowledge, represent perspectives that are based on limited experience and understanding. Ethical injunctions, moral laws, and codes may effectively control and inhibit antisocial behavior and they may even be grounded in some rather fundamental aspects of our human nature. But being permeated with *avidyā*, with a consciousness of separation and distinction, they are necessarily partial and incomplete.

We have seen now some of the epistemological and axiological implications of the multileveled ontology of Advaita Vedānta—which affirms three levels of being: absolute being, practical or empirical being, and illusory being, with the first of these alone being fully real. It follows from this affirmation that reality is unknowable by the standards of ordinary intellectual activity or reason. Reason can point the way to reality, but it cannot disclose or demonstrate it. It also follows from this multileveled ontology that we are never able to explain fully the nature of our ordinary experience. One cannot reason across incommensurable levels. One cannot explain the "why" of existence. All intellectual, rational, scientific knowledge is touched with a special kind of ignorance (*avidyā*) or incompleteness. This knowledge is necessarily a lower knowledge (*aparā vidyā*). It is justified nevertheless when it is accepted in its own terms and does not have pretensions to ultimacy or finality. Another implication for knowledge that follows from the Advaitin's ontology is that an insight into reality does not provide one with any special privileged knowledge of the world. Reality does not admit of multiplicity and cannot give one any extraordinary or magical knowledge of, or control over, the forces operative in empirical being. Insight removes ignorance and provides an understanding that is qualitatively different in kind from rational or scientific knowing. Intuitive understanding has its unique domain and reason has its appropriate place.

Reality is value, then, and man's highest good is to realize his identity with it. This identity, this state of absolute being, is a state of complete freedom (*mokṣa*); it is utter peace and blessedness. If the highest value for man is to achieve this state of freedom, then on the level of empirical experience, it must be affirmed that the end justifies the means, when the end is the attainment of freedom. This leads to a standard teaching technique in Indian philosophy that communicates the contents of insight by appealing to the level of understanding of the disciple.

The last axiological implication that we called attention to concerns the status of all value judgments: they necessarily are partial and incomplete. Reality transcends all value discriminations and condemns all judgments based on separative distinctions to relativity.

Before closing, let us step outside of the system of Advaita Vedānta and ask: Does it make sense? Is it a meaningful ontology? The answer, I think, is yes—provided one is willing to admit the possibility of the Advaitin's nondual spiritual experience. For one unable to admit this, the system will inevitably be a piece of pernicious nonsense. But if the experience is admitted (and I see no reason to assume that seers and sages throughout history were just deluded or mad) it does seem to me that Advaita Vedānta is a remarkable and bold philosophical achievement.

Claiming that reality is undifferentiated, a fullness of consciousness and being, and it then asserts that we cannot claim an ultimate or independent reality for our empirical experience. In Western philosophy and religion we tend to be somewhat schizophrenic about this. We want a God who is "really real" and at the same time we want him to create a wholly real world that is distinct from him. We want a Christ who is entirely human and entirely divine. We want a God who is "good," yet who somehow permits evil to flourish. I need not, I am sure, point out the many insolvable theological problems that this desire has given rise to. But Advaita Vedānta will have none of these problems. It uncompromisingly accepts the implications of experience. We cannot know reality, it claims (and no doubt rightly), and hence we cannot establish causal relations between the real and the empirical. We cannot know fully or completely empirical being, Advaita claims (and again no doubt rightly) and similarly we cannot establish with finality anything in the domain of morality. Philosophy, according to Advaita, must be grounded in experience, not in mere speculation, and the philosophy of Advaita Vedānta is clearly so grounded.

NOTES

1. *Saṁbandha Vārtika*, as quoted by N. K. Devaraja in *An Introduction to Śaṁkara's Theory of Knowledge* (Delhi: Motilal Banarsidass, 1962), p. 16.

2. *Brahmasūtrabhāṣya* 3. 2. 22 in *The Vedānta-Sūtras with the Commentary of Śaṅkarācārya*, trans. George Thibaut. Sacred Books of the East, vols. 34 and 38, ed. Max Müller (Oxford: The Clarendon Press, 1890 and 1896).

3. *Kena Upaniṣad* (Hume trans.) 2. 3.

4. *Bṛhadāraṇyakopaniṣadbhāṣya* 3. 5. 1.

5. Ibid., 1. 4. 10.

WIDENER COLLEGE
WOLFGRAM
LIBRARY
CHESTER, PA.